Book 1: General Financial Planning Principles, Professional Conduct, and Regulation

Financial Education — KAPLAN UNIVERSITY — SCHOOL OF PROFESSIONAL AND CONTINUING EDUCATION

At press time, this edition contains the most complete and accurate information currently available. Due to the nature of advanced designation examinations, however, information may have been added recently to the actual test that does not appear in this edition. Please contact the publisher to verify that you have the most current edition.

This publication is designed to provide accurate and authoritative information in regard to the subject matter covered. It is sold with the understanding that the publisher is not engaged in rendering legal, accounting, or other professional services. If legal advice or other expert assistance is required, the services of a competent professional should be sought.

KAPLAN UNIVERSITY SCHOOL OF PROFESSIONAL AND CONTINUING EDUCATION FINANCIAL EDUCATION REVIEW FOR THE CFP® CERTIFICATION EXAMINATION BOOK 1: GENERAL FINANCIAL PLANNING PRINCIPLES, PROFESSIONAL CONDUCT, AND REGULATION 2017
©2017 Kaplan, Inc. All rights reserved.

CLU®, ChFC®, Registered Health Underwriter®, RHU®, REBC® Chartered Life Underwriter®, Chartered Financial Consultant®, Registered Employee Benefits Consultant®, Chartered Advisor for Senior Living™, and CASL™ are registered trademarks of The American College.

CPCU®, ARM®, and AIC® are registered trademarks of the American Institute for CPCU and the Insurance Institute of America.

CFP®, CERTIFIED FINANCIAL PLANNER™, and CFP® are certification marks or registered certification marks of Certified Financial Planner Board of Standards, Inc.

Published by Kaplan Financial Education

Printed in the United States of America.

ISBN: 978-1-4754-4473-5

Preface

PRODUCTS AND SERVICES FOR THE CFP® EXAM

KAPLAN FINANCIAL EDUCATION REVIEW COURSES FOR THE CFP® EXAM

Kaplan Financial Education offers several options to meet the diverse needs of candidates.

THE LIVE REVIEW COURSE

Instruction in both the traditional and virtual classroom programs consists mainly of teaching substantive material and helping students master both the knowledge and application of topics that they will likely encounter on the exam. Material is also presented integrating CFP Board's Job Task Domains with exam topics. The course includes working through various types of problems to ensure that the substantive materials taught can be applied to exam-like questions. Students also receive instruction in actual exam-management techniques.

Many videos are available to Live Review students. These videos help students study important CFP® Exam topics prior to the Live Review. In preparation for the Live Review, students also have access to videos that help them with case studies and the Kaplan Financial Education mock exam.

Traditional Classroom Program

Kaplan Financial Education offers the Traditional Classroom Program in major metropolitan areas across the country. The Four-Day Review is an intensive program consisting of over 30 hours of instruction conducted, in most cases, Thursday through Sunday.

The Virtual Classroom Program

Kaplan Financial Education's Virtual Review is an instructor-led, web-based program that provides all the benefits of a classroom review from the convenience of the student's home or office. This program format is a great option for those who have access to the web and prefer not to incur the expense of travel. This course is an intensive program consisting of 33 hours of instruction in 11 three-hour classes. Students receive real-time interaction with their instructor and have access to a recorded playback option. Playbacks are available for review until the first day of the CFP® Exam.

LIVE REVIEW STUDY TOOLS

In-Class Guide

The In-Class Guide is an easy-to-use Live Review class companion with study notes to help keep students organized during and after class.

Diagnostic Exam

Available only to Live Review students, the Diagnostic Exam allows students to identify areas of strength and weakness prior to studying for the CFP® Exam. This study aid allows students to tailor their study plans to the areas identified on a report provided once the Diagnostic Exam is completed.

Pre-Review Videos

Available on demand, pre-review videos provide additional instruction for those taking the CFP® Exam. Viewing these videos early in the study process helps students understand how CFP Board may test topics.

Case Videos

A considerable number of points for the CFP® Exam are case-related, so case preparation is critical. Students can develop important case analysis skills with this on-demand study tool.

Mock Exam Videos

Students learn how to approach the CFP® Exam with this video that provides exam strategies to be used as they take the online mock exam and the national CFP® Exam.

BOOKS 1–6

Books 1–6 contain complete reference outlines that give detailed coverage of each of the six tested areas of the CFP® Exam. Each book contains examples, illustrations, and an index. Each book has been updated to reflect 2017 law and inflation adjustments available at date of printing.

BOOK 7—FINANCIAL PLANNING CASE STUDIES

Book 7—Financial Planning Case Studies is designed to prepare students for the comprehensive cases included on the exam. This valuable study tool provides the exam candidate with 12 comprehensive cases, item sets, and mini-cases that test students' knowledge and application of the exam topics. The answers and explanations for each multiple-choice question are provided, and the text has been updated to reflect 2017 law and inflation adjustments available at the date of printing. Students who have used the *Financial Planning Case Studies* have said that this book is a must to be prepared for the exam.

MOCK EXAM AND SOLUTIONS

Mock Exam and Solutions simulates the six-hour comprehensive CFP® Exam. Much like the actual exam, this online exam is divided into two sessions with a three-hour time limit for each session. Each session contains multiple-choice questions, item sets, and comprehensive cases. This mock exam serves as a diagnostic tool useful in identifying a student's areas of strength and weakness and can be used to help them focus on topics that they find more difficult. The mock exam is also updated to reflect 2017 law and inflation adjustments.

UNDERSTANDING YOUR FINANCIAL CALCULATOR

Understanding Your Financial Calculator is a book designed to assist students in gaining proficiency in using a financial calculator to work through problems they may encounter on the exam. In addition to helping master the keystrokes for the financial calculator, it is also designed to assist students with the underlying financial theory of these problems. All calculations are worked out step by step, showing keystrokes and displays for several of the most popular financial calculators. For more information, contact a Kaplan academic advisor at 1-877-446-9034 or advisor@kaplan.com.

EXAM PREP/REVIEW (EPR) ONLINE REVIEW QBANK

Designed to be used in conjunction with Books 1–7 and the mock exam, the EPR online review QBank is an interactive software product of high cognitive level questions designed to give students practice in answering questions relating to content most likely tested on the CFP® Exam. There are two cognitive levels of questions in the EPR QBank:

- Analyze & Apply QBank: higher cognitive exam-type level questions that challenge students studying for the CFP® Exam.
- Recall & Review QBank: questions that reinforce knowledge that CFP® Exam candidates should have at a base level. It is intended to be used for the review of concepts learned in CFP® Exam base courses or as a refresher for those students challenging the exam.

Students can create customized, timed practice quizzes from the six topics tested on the CFP® Exam. All practice quizzes are scored and allow students to analyze their competencies by topical areas. Customized quizzes may be saved for future reference.

CORE LECTURE VIDEOS

Students can reinforce their knowledge and application of the core concepts of the CFP® Exam with online videos. Explanations and examples of these concepts are presented in an easy-to-understand manner by subject matter experts.

EXAM TIPS VIDEOS

Students have the opportunity to watch innovative videos that provide strategies and tips for CFP® Exam preparation. Video topics include CFP Board domains and topics, the CFP® Exam format, how to approach multiple-choice questions and case studies, Kaplan Financial Education tools available for exam success, and what to expect on exam day.

FROM THE PUBLISHER

This text is intended as the basis for preparation for the CFP® Exam, either as self-study or as part of a review course. The material is organized according to the six functional areas tested on the exam and is presented in an outline format that includes examples and illustrations that help candidates quickly comprehend the material.

The material is organized into six manageable study books and a comprehensive case book:

- *Book 1—General Financial Planning Principles, Professional Conduct, and Regulation*
- *Book 2—Risk Management, Insurance, and Employee Benefits Planning*
- *Book 3—Investment Planning*
- *Book 4—Tax Planning*
- *Book 5—Retirement Savings and Income Planning*
- *Book 6—Estate Planning*
- *Book 7—Financial Planning Case Studies*

We are indebted to Certified Financial Planner Board of Standards, Inc. for permission to reproduce and adapt their publications and other materials.

Wishing you success on the exam,

Kaplan Financial Education

CONTRIBUTING AUTHORS

- Kathy L. Berlin
  - —Senior Content Specialist, Kaplan Financial Education
  - —Successfully passed CFP® Certification Examination
  - —Certified Public Accountant (Inactive)
  - —BA from Loyola University of New Orleans, Louisiana
  - —Former CFO of a large nonprofit organization
  - —Co-author of Kaplan Financial Education's *Personal Financial Planning Cases and Applications*, *5th–8th Editions* textbook and instructor manual
  - —Co-author of Kaplan University/Financial Education's *Personal Financial Planning Cases and Applications*, *9th Edition* textbook and instructor manual
  - —Co-author of Kaplan Financial Education's *Personal Financial Planning Theory and Practice*, *4th–7th Editions* textbook and instructor manual
  - —Co-author of Kaplan University/Financial Education's *Personal Financial Planning Theory and Practice*, *8th–9th Editions*, textbook and instructor manual
  - —Co-author of the *Kaplan Schweser Review for the CFP® Certification Examination*, *9th–14th Editions*
  - —Co-author of the *Kaplan Schweser Review for the CFP® Certification Examination*, *July–November 2010, March–November 2011, and 2012–2013 Exams*
  - —Co-author of Kaplan University/Financial Education's *CFP® Exam Prep Review Books 1–7, 2014–2017*
  - —Co-author of the *Kaplan University/Kaplan Schweser Certification Examination Education Program*, *4th–11th Editions* materials
  - —Co-author of Kaplan University/Financial Education's *CFP® Exam Required Education Course Materials 2014–2017*

- Glen Kramer, MSF, CRPC®, GCPM, PMP®, CFP®
  - —Senior Content Specialist, Kaplan Financial Education
  - —BS in Economics from University of Wisconsin–Stevens Point
  - —MSF from Kaplan University
  - —Over 12 years of experience in the insurance and securities business
  - —Former General Securities Representative
  - —Former Life and Health Insurance Licensed Sales Representative in Arizona, Nevada, and Wisconsin
  - —Co-author of Kaplan Financial Education's *Personal Financial Planning Cases and Applications*, *7th and 8th Editions* textbook and instructor manual
  - —Co-author of Kaplan University/Financial Education's *Personal Financial Planning Cases and Applications*, *9th Edition* textbook and instructor manual

—Co-author of Kaplan Financial Education's *Personal Financial Planning Theory and Practice*, *7th Edition* textbook and instructor manual

—Co-author of Kaplan University/Financial Education's *Personal Financial Planning Theory and Practice*, *8th–9th Editions*, textbook and instructor manual

—Co-author of the *Kaplan Schweser Review for the CFP® Certification Examination*, *March–November 2011, and 2012–2013 Exams*

—Co-author of Kaplan University/Financial Education's CFP® *Exam Prep Review Books 1–7, 2014–2017*

—Co-author of the *Kaplan University/Kaplan Schweser Certification Examination Education Program*, *8th–11th Editions* materials

—Co-author of Kaplan University/Financial Education's CFP® *Exam Required Education Course Materials 2014–2017*

■ Michael Long, CLU®, ChFC®, CFP®

—Senior Content Specialist, Kaplan Financial Education

—Over 25 years' experience in insurance and securities as a sales manager, classroom instructor, product manager, and advanced underwriting consultant

—BS in Business Administration, Indiana State University

—Co-author of Kaplan Financial Education's *Personal Financial Planning Cases and Applications*, *6th–8th Editions* textbook and instructor manual

—Co-author of Kaplan University/Financial Education's *Personal Financial Planning Cases and Applications*, *9th Edition* textbook and instructor manual

—Co-author of Kaplan Financial Education's *Personal Financial Planning Theory and Practice*, *6th–7th Editions* textbook and instructor manual

—Co-author of Kaplan University/Financial Education's *Personal Financial Planning Theory and Practice*, *8th–9th Editions*, textbook and instructor manual

—Co-author of the *Schweser Review for the CFP® Certification Examination*, *13th–14th Editions*

—Co-author of the *Kaplan Schweser Review for the CFP® Certification Examination*, *July–November 2010 Exams, and 2012–2013 Exams*

—Co-author of Kaplan University/Financial Education's CFP® *Exam Prep Review Books 1–7, 2014–2017*

—Co-author of the *Kaplan University/Kaplan Schweser Certification Examination Education Program*, *8th–11th Editions* materials

—Co-author of Kaplan University/Financial Education's CFP® *Exam Required Education Course Materials 2014–2017*

■ James Maher, MBA, CLU®, ChFC®, CFP®

—Senior Content Specialist, Kaplan Financial Education

—Former securities and insurance instructor, Kaplan Financial

—Former Insurance Representative–General Securities

—BBA from Florida International University

—MBA from Kaplan University

QUESTION TYPES

The examination consis[...]
stand-alone questions th[...]
included are item set an[...]
questions. A portion of [...]
both of the two exam se[...]
needed to answer these [...]
several pages long, maki[...]
questions.

The stand-alone questic[...]
area of financial planni[...]
questions, meaning tha[...]
might integrate investn[...]
ability to analyze fact si[...]

TIME AND TIME [...]

There are six hours of [...]

- Two 3-hour session[...]
- Approximately 17[...]
- Case questions, av[...]

PASS RATES

Student pass rates hav[...]
professional exam witl[...]
prepared for all the to[...]

—Co-author of Kaplan Financial Education's *Personal Financial Planning Cases and Applications*, 6th–8th Editions textbook and instructor manual

—Co-author of Kaplan University/Financial Education's *Personal Financial Planning Cases and Applications*, 9th Edition textbook and instructor manual

—Co-author of Kaplan Financial Education's *Personal Financial Planning Theory and Practice*, 5th–7th Editions textbook and instructor manual

—Co-author of Kaplan University/Financial Education's *Personal Financial Planning Theory and Practice*, 8th–9th Editions, textbook and instructor manual

—Co-author of the *Kaplan Schweser Review for the CFP® Certification Examination, 12th–14th Editions*

—Co-author of the *Kaplan Schweser Review for the CFP® Certification Examination, July–November 2010, March–November 2011, and 2012–2013 Exams*

—Co-author of Kaplan University/Financial Education's *CFP® Exam Prep Review Books 1–7, 2014–2017*

—Co-author of the *Kaplan University/Kaplan Schweser Certification Examination Education Program, 6th–11th Editions* materials

—Co-author of Kaplan University/Financial Education's *CFP® Exam Required Education Course Materials 2014–2017*

■ Cindy R. Riecke, MSF, CLU®, ChFC®, CFP®

—Senior Director, Kaplan Financial Education

—BS in Business Administration from Louisiana State University in Baton Rouge, Louisiana

—MSF from Kaplan University

—Member of the Financial Planning Association

Former Director of Marketing Development for an international insurance and financial services company

—Co-author of Kaplan Financial Education's *Personal Financial Planning Cases and Applications*, 5th–8th Editions textbook and instructor manual

—Co-author of Kaplan University/Financial Education's *Personal Financial Planning Cases and Applications*, 9th Edition textbook and instructor manual

—Co-author of Kaplan Financial Education's *Personal Financial Planning Theory and Practice*, 4th–7th Editions textbook and instructor manual

—Co-author of Kaplan University/Financial Education's *Personal Financial Planning Theory and Practice*, 8th–9th Editions, textbook and instructor manual

—Co-author of the *Kaplan Schweser Review for the CFP® Certification Examination, 9th–14th Editions*

—Co-author of the *Kaplan Schweser Review for the CFP® Certification Examination, July–November 2010, March–November 2011, and 2012–2013 Exams*

—Co-author of Kaplan University/Financial Education's *CFP® Exam Prep Review Books 1–7, 2014–2017*

ABOUT THE CFP® EXA

EXAMINATION PROCED

Read carefully the procedures o
The section entitled "CFP® Ce

- dates of examinations;
- alternate test dates and tes
- fees for the examination;
- scheduling confirmations;
- withdrawal from the exam
- medical emergencies;
- items to bring to the exam
- examination misconduct;
- examination scoring;
- score reports;
- pass score;
- reexamination procedure
- review and appeals.

A copy of the *Guide to CFP*®
address:

Certifiec

DATE GIVEN

The exam is administered a
over a five-day window in

It is the student's responsib
exam.

For updates and informati
deadlines, and so forth, pl

For updates to Kaplan Fir
inflation-adjusted tax rat
Prep Review dashboard.

4. Developing the Recommendation(s)

A) Evaluate alternatives to meet the client's goals and objectives
   1) Sensitivity analysis (e.g., factors outside of client control)
B) Consult with other professionals as appropriate
C) Develop recommendations considering:
   1) Client attitudes, values and beliefs
   2) Behavioral finance issues (e.g., anchoring, overconfidence, recency)
   3) Their interdependence
D) Document recommendations

5. Communicating the Recommendation(s)

A) Present financial plan and provide guidance
   1) Goals
   2) Assumptions
   3) Observations and findings
   4) Alternatives
   5) Recommendations
B) Obtain feedback from the client and revise the recommendations as appropriate
C) Provide documentation of plan recommendations and any additional disclosures
D) Verify client acceptance of recommendations

6. Implementing the Recommendation(s)

A) Create a prioritized implementation plan with timeline
B) Directly or indirectly implement the recommendations
C) Coordinate and share information, as authorized, with others
D) Define monitoring responsibilities with the client (e.g., explain what will be monitored, frequency of monitoring, communication method(s))

7. Monitoring the Recommendation(s)

A) Discuss and evaluate changes in the client's personal circumstances (e.g., aging issues, change in employment)
B) Review the performance and progress of the plan
C) Review and evaluate changes in the legal, tax and economic environments
D) Make recommendations to accommodate changed circumstances
E) Review scope of work and redefine engagement as appropriate
F) Provide ongoing client support (e.g., guidance, education)

8. Practicing within Professional and Regulatory Standards

A) Adhere to CFP Board's *Standards of Professional Conduct*
B) Manage practice risk (e.g., documentation, monitor client noncompliance with recommendations)
C) Maintain awareness of and comply with regulatory and legal guidelines

CONTEXTUAL VARIABLES

In addition to the Principal Knowledge Topics, other important variables are to be considered when dealing with specific financial planning situations. These are referred to as "Contextual Variables" and are used as part of content development for the CFP® Certification Examination or other case-based scenarios.

More specifically, financial planning situations require the application of financial planning knowledge for different types of clients. Important client details to consider as part of financial planning situations are:

- **Family Status** (traditional family, single parent, same-sex couples, blended families, widowhood)
- **Net Worth** (ultra-high net worth, high net worth, mass affluent, emerging affluent, mass market)
- **Income Level** (high, medium, low)
- **Life or Professional Stage** (student, starting a career, career transition, pre-retirement, retirement)
- **Other Circumstances** (health issues, divorce, change of employment status, aging parents, special needs children)

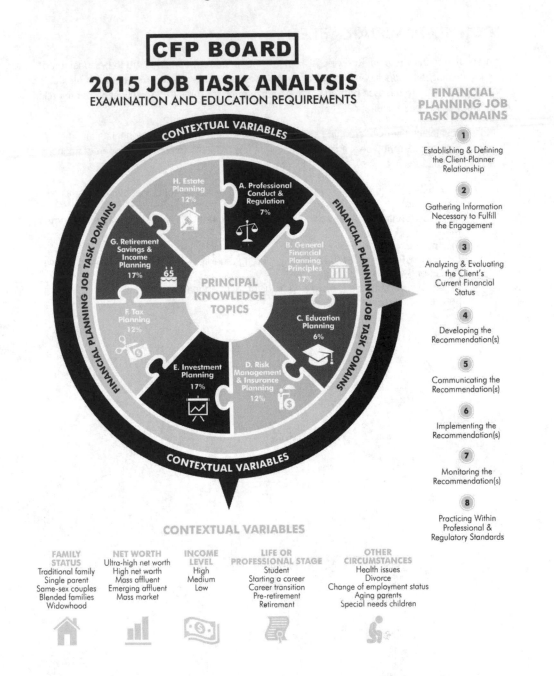

CERTIFIED FINANCIAL PLANNER BOARD OF STANDARDS, INC.

2015 Principal Knowledge Topics (72 Topics)

The following Principal Knowledge Topics are based on the results of CFP Board's 2015 Job Analysis Study.

The Principal Knowledge Topics serve as the blueprint for the March 2016 and later administrations of the CFP® Certification Examination. Each exam question will be linked to one of the following Principal Knowledge Topics, in the approximate percentages indicated following the general category headings.

The Principal Knowledge Topics serve as a curricular framework and also represent subject topics that CFP Board accepts for continuing education credit, effective January 2016.

Eight Principal Knowledge Topic Categories

- **A. Professional Conduct and Regulation** (7%)
- **B. General Financial Planning Principles** (17%)
- **C. Education Planning** (6%)
- **D. Risk Management and Insurance Planning** (12%)
- **E. Investment Planning** (17%)
- **F. Tax Planning** (12%)
- **G. Retirement Savings and Income Planning** (17%)
- **H. Estate Planning** (12%)

A. Professional Conduct and Regulation

A.1.   CFP Board's Code of Ethics and Professional Responsibility and Rules of Conduct

A.2.   CFP Board's Financial Planning Practice Standards

A.3.   CFP Board's Disciplinary Rules and Procedures

A.4.   Function, purpose, and regulation of financial institutions

A.5.   Financial services regulations and requirements

A.6.   Consumer protection laws

A.7.   Fiduciary

Professional Conduct & Regulation

B. General Principles of Financial Planning

General Financial Planning Principles

B.8.	Financial planning process
B.9.	Financial statements
B.10.	Cash flow management
B.11.	Financing strategies
B.12.	Economic concepts
B.13.	Time value of money concepts and calculations
B.14.	Client and planner attitudes, values, biases and behavioral finance
B.15.	Principles of communication and counseling
B.16.	Debt management

C. Education Planning

Education Planning

C.17.	Education needs analysis
C.18.	Education savings vehicles
C.19.	Financial aid
C.20.	Gift/income tax strategies
C.21.	Education financing

D. Risk Management and Insurance Planning

Risk Management & Insurance Planning

D.22.	Principles of risk and insurance
D.23.	Analysis and evaluation of risk exposures
D.24.	Health insurance and health care cost management (individual)
D.25.	Disability income insurance (individual)
D.26.	Long-term care insurance (individual)
D.27.	Annuities
D.28.	Life insurance (individual)
D.29.	Business uses of insurance
D.30.	Insurance needs analysis
D.31.	Insurance policy and company selection
D.32.	Property and casualty insurance

E. Investment Planning

E.33.	Characteristics, uses and taxation of investment vehicles
E.34.	Types of investment risk
E.35.	Quantitative investment concepts
E.36.	Measures of investment returns
E.37.	Asset allocation and portfolio diversification
E.38.	Bond and stock valuation concepts
E.39.	Portfolio development and analysis
E.40.	Investment strategies
E.41.	Alternative investments

Investment Planning

F. Tax Planning

F.42.	Fundamental tax law
F.43	Income tax fundamentals and calculations
F.44.	Characteristics and income taxation of business entities
F.45.	Income taxation of trusts and estates
F.46.	Alternative minimum tax (AMT)
F.47.	Tax reduction/management techniques
F.48.	Tax consequences of property transactions
F.49.	Passive activity and at-risk rules
F.50.	Tax implications of special circumstances
F.51.	Charitable/philanthropic contributions and deductions

Tax Planning

G. Retirement Savings and Income Planning

G.52.	Retirement needs analysis
G.53.	Social Security and Medicare
G.54.	Medicaid
G.55.	Types of retirement plans
G.56.	Qualified plan rules and options
G.57.	Other tax-advantaged retirement plans
G.58.	Regulatory considerations
G.59.	Key factors affecting plan selection for businesses

Retirement Savings & Income Planning

G.60.   Distribution rules and taxation

G.61.   Retirement income and distribution strategies

G.62.   Business succession planning

H. Estate Planning

H.63.   Characteristics and consequences of property titling

H.64.   Strategies to transfer property

H.65.   Estate planning documents

H.66.   Gift and estate tax compliance and tax calculation

H.67.   Sources for estate liquidity

H.68.   Types, features, and taxation of trusts

H.69.   Marital deduction

H.70.   Intra-family and other business transfer techniques

H.71.   Postmortem estate planning techniques

H.72.   Estate planning for non-traditional relationships

Contextual Variables

In addition to the Principal Knowledge Topics, other important variables are to be considered when dealing with specific financial planning situations. These are referred to as "Contextual Variables" and are used as part of content development for the CFP® Certification Examination or other case-based scenarios.

More specifically, financial planning situations require the application of financial planning knowledge for different types of clients. Important client details to consider as part of financial planning situations are:

- **Family Status** (traditional family, single parent, same-sex couples, blended families, widowhood)
- **Net Worth** (ultra-high net worth, high net worth, mass affluent, emerging affluent, mass market)
- **Income Level** (high, medium, low)
- **Life or Professional Stage** (student, starting a career, career transition, pre-retirement, retirement)
- **Other Circumstances** (health issues, divorce, change of employment status, aging parents, special needs children)

Introduction   xxv

CFP Board 2015 Principal Knowledge Topics (cont.)   Page 5 of 5

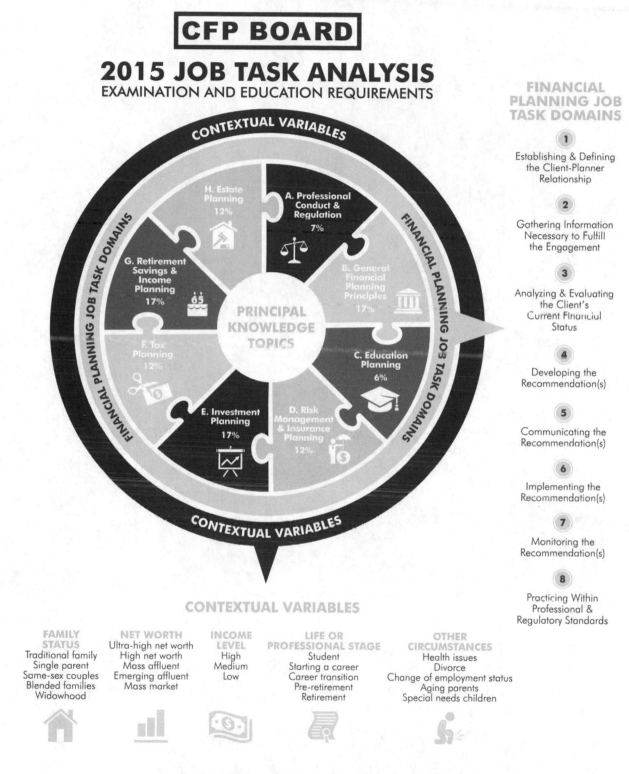

Table of Contents

TABLE OF EXHIBITS

TABLE OF APPENDICES

BOOK

1

General Financial Planning Principles, Professional Conduct, and Regulation

I.   FINANCIAL PLANNING PROCESS

CFP Board Principal Knowledge Topic B.8.

A.   WHAT IS FINANCIAL PLANNING?

1. *Financial planning* is defined in CFP Board's Standards of Professional Conduct as "the process of determining whether and how an individual can meet life goals through the proper management of financial resources."

2. The subject matter of financial planning is incorporated into the financial planning process when financial planning takes place. According to The Standards of Professional Conduct, these subject matter areas include:

   a. Financial statement preparation and analysis (including cash flow analysis/planning and budgeting)

   b. Insurance planning and risk management

   c. Employee benefits planning

   d. Investment planning

   e. Income tax planning

   f. Retirement planning

   g. Estate planning

B.   WHAT ARE THE MATERIAL ELEMENTS OF FINANCIAL PLANNING?

1. A number of The Standards of Professional Conduct's ethical obligations apply only when a CFP® professional is engaged in financial planning or material elements of the financial planning process.

2. The CFP Board Rules of Conduct must be followed by any person allowed to use the CFP® marks, regardless of his nature of employment, title, role, or compensation structure.

3. Whether financial planning exists or the material elements of financial planning are present is not always clear.

4. According to CFP Board, some considerations that may assist in determining if this is the case include, but are not limited to the following:

   a. the client's (not the CFP® professional's) expectations, understanding, and intent by engaging the professional—therefore, a CFP® professional's messaging to clients should not create confusion regarding whether the certificant is providing financial planning services (if a client, based on the CFP® professional's messaging, believes that the CFP® professional is providing financial planning services, in all likelihood he is);

   b. the degree to which multiple financial planning subject areas are addressed (the greater the scope the analysis, the more likely the activities will be considered material elements of financial planning);

    c. the comprehensiveness of the data-gathering regarding multiple aspects of a client's financial situation (the more detailed the data-gathering for multiple aspects of a client's circumstances, the more likely the service will be considered financial planning);

    d. the breadth and depth of the recommendations (the more comprehensive the recommendations, the more likely the activities will be considered financial planning); and

    e. providing investment advisory services as defined by the SEC will be considered financial planning.

5. Activities CFP Board may consider *not* to be material elements of the financial planning process include the following:

    a. Completing paperwork to open a brokerage account

    b. Acting as an order-taker for brokerage services

    c. Engaging solely in sales activity related to insurance products

    d. Acting as a mortgage broker without providing any other financial services

    e. Completing tax returns without providing any other financial services

    f. Teaching a financial class or continuing education program

Be aware that, per CFP Board, these preliminary guidelines are examples and not an all-inclusive list.

6. Financial planning letter of engagement (see sample in Appendix)

    a. Defines the legal relationship between the financial planner and the client

    b. The CFP® certificant and the client should reduce the agreement to writing and, in this Agreement, specify:

        1.) the parties to the Agreement;

        2.) the date of the Agreement and its duration;

        3.) how and on what terms each party can terminate the Agreement; and

        4.) the services to be provided as part of the Agreement.

C. CFP® CERTIFICATION EXAM JOB TASK DOMAINS

You must thoroughly understand these job task domains. Questions on the CFP® exam will test the CFP Board principal topics in the context of these eight domains. You will be required to not only understand the topics and their applications but also know the best actions a CFP® professional should take and when. These types of questions are presented throughout the Kaplan exam prep/review books, the online mock exams, and the exam prep/review practice Analyze and Apply QBank.

1. CFP Board job task domains:

    a. Domain 1 – Establishing and defining the client-planner relationship

    b. Domain 2 – Gathering information necessary to fulfill the engagement

    c. Domain 3 – Analyzing and evaluating the client's current financial status

      d.   Domain 4 – Developing the recommendations

      e.   Domain 5 – Communicating the recommendations

      f.   Domain 6 – Implementing the recommendations

      g.   Domain 7 – Monitoring the recommendations

      h.   Domain 8 – Practicing within professional and regulatory standards

D. SIX-STEP FINANCIAL PLANNING PROCESS

1. The financial planning process is based on the eight CFP Board job task domains as illustrated below.

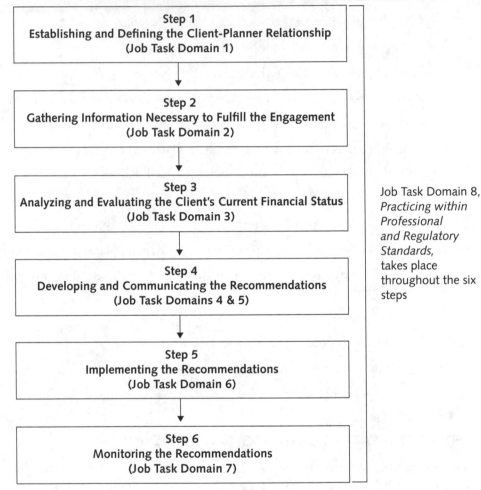

2. Step 1: Establishing and defining the client-planner relationship (*Domain 1*)

    a. Activities involved:

        1.)   Identify the client (individual, family, business, organization)

        2.)   Discuss the financial planning process

        3.)   Explain the scope of services offered

        4.)   Assess and communicate ability to meet the client's needs and expectations

        5.)   Identify and disclose conflicts of interest in client relationships

6.) Discuss the responsibilities of the client, CFP® professional, and other parties involved

7.) Define and document the scope of the engagement with the client

8.) Provide client disclosures

    a.) Regulatory disclosure

    b.) Compensation arrangements and associated potential conflicts of interest

---

ANALYZE AND APPLY

George and Betty Steiner are a married couple, both age 62, with two adult daughters, Rachel and Katherine. The Steiners have recently received a considerable inheritance and, because they own a modest amount of assets, feel they should have a formal financial plan so that their finances are managed more appropriately. In their financial plan, they would also like to include a means to leave an inheritance to Rachel but, since they have been estranged from Katherine for many years, choose not to include her in their wills. They would also like to leave legacies to their six grandchildren. They have contacted Marie, a CFP® professional, for some financial planning assistance. The focus of Marie's practice is primarily retirement planning, although in the past she has worked with other financial planners to create comprehensive financial plans. During the initial meeting with the Steiners, Marie realizes that Katherine is also one of her financial planning clients, and last month she met with Katherine to discuss options for a future inheritance from her parents. Which of the following statements regarding Marie's obligations at this stage of the client-planner relationship is(are) CORRECT?

1. Marie should assess and communicate her ability to meet the client's needs and expectations.
2. Marie should resolve the potential conflict of interest as a result of her working relationship with Katherine.
3. Marie should identify who her client(s) will be and define the scope of the relationship with the client(s) before proceeding.
4. Marie should ask the Steiners to provide information concerning their current wills so she can begin developing appropriate recommendations.

A. 3 only
B. 1 and 2
C. 2 and 4
D. 1, 2, and 3

Answer: D. Statement 1 is correct. Because estate planning is not Marie's primary area of expertise, she should assess and communicate her ability to meet the clients' needs and expectations while establishing and defining the client-planner relationship. Statement 2 is correct. Marie's working relationship with Katherine creates a potential conflict of interest because Katherine, as part of her financial planning process, is discussing a future inheritance she will likely never receive. Statement 3 is correct because Marie's potential clients include the Steiners, their daughter, Rachel, and the grandchildren, all of whom may have differing needs and expectations. Statement 4 is incorrect. Marie should not ask the couple for information regarding their wills until she has established and defined the client-planner relationship and has resolved the potential conflict of interest with Katherine. (Domain 1 – Establishing and Defining the Client-Planner Relationship)

b. CFP Board, under Rule of Conduct 1.2, requires CFP® certificants to make the following disclosures *verbally or in writing* before entering into an agreement to provide financial planning services. These disclosures are usually made at the first or second client meeting.

   1.) The obligations and responsibilities of each party under the agreement with respect to:

   a.) defining goals, needs, and objectives;

   b.) gathering and providing appropriate data;

   c.) examining the result of the current course of action without changes;

   d.) the formulation of any recommended actions;

   e.) implementation responsibilities; and

   f.) monitoring responsibilities.

   2.) Compensation that any party to the agreement will or could receive under the terms of the agreement

   3.) Terms under which the agreement permits the certificant to offer proprietary products

   4.) Terms under which the certificant will use other entities to meet any of the agreement's obligations

c. CFP Board requires a *written agreement* by the CFP® certificant or his employer *after* the scope of the engagement has been mutually defined by the CFP® professional and the client, and *prior to* the professional providing financial planning or material elements of financial planning to a client. The following information and disclosures must be *in writing*:

   1.) The *parties* to the agreement

   2.) The *date and duration* of the agreement

   3.) *How and on what terms each party can end the agreement*

   4.) The *services to be provided* under the agreement

5.) A precise and understandable *description of the compensation arrangements* being offered

6.) A summary of *likely conflicts of interest* between the client and the certificant, certificant's employer or any affiliates or third parties, or interests of the certificant, certificant's employer or any affiliates or third parties that *appear to conflict* with those of the client

7.) Any information regarding the certificant or the certificant's employer that could realistically be expected to considerably *influence the client's decision* to engage the certificant or that the client might reasonably want to know in establishing the scope and nature of the relationship (this includes information about the certificant's area of expertise)

8.) *Contact information* for the certificant and, if applicable, the certificant's employer

d. The requirement that information be disclosed in writing depends upon whether an agreement to provide financial planning services has been entered into by the planner and the client.

1.) Prior to an agreement: may be disclosed verbally or in writing

2.) With an agreement: must be disclosed in writing

ANALYZE AND APPLY

David has decided to retain Lucas, a CFP® certificant, as his financial planner. They discuss the services Lucas will provide and other details regarding the nature of their relationship. CFP Board requires a written agreement by Lucas detailing which of the following elements?

1. The date and duration of the agreement
2. A general description of the compensation arrangements being offered
3. Terms under which the agreement permits the certificant to offer proprietary products
4. Terms under which the certificant will use other entities to meet any of the agreement's obligations

A. 1 only
B. 1 and 2
C. 2 and 3
D. 1, 2, and 3

Answer: A. An element that must be in writing addresses the date and duration of the agreement. A *precise and understandable* description of the compensation arrangements being offered, not merely one that is general, must be included in a written agreement. The terms under which the CFP® professional will use other entities to meet any of the agreement's obligations may be communicated verbally or in writing, as can the terms under which the certificant will use other entities to meet any of the obligations of the agreement. (Domain 1 – Establishing and Defining the Client-Planner Relationship)

3. Step 2: Gathering information necessary to fulfill the engagement (*Domain 2*)

a. Obtain information from client through interview/questionnaire regarding financial resources and obligations

b. Determine client's personal and financial goals, needs, and priorities

    1.) The planner should encourage the client to:

        a.) identify financial needs and set goals accordingly; and

        b.) prioritize multiple goals as financial resources may prove insufficient to fund them all.

    2.) Examples of questions the financial planner may ask to assist the client when establishing goals and expectations, identifying needs, and developing priorities

        a.) What level and type of education would you like your children to have?

        b.) Do you own a business, and have you made provisions for someone to succeed you in ownership of that business? If so, what are the provisions?

        c.) Are you charitably inclined and, if so, what charities do you favor?

        d.) What provisions have you made for your minor children in the event you and your spouse die?

        e.) Have you been previously married, and are there children from that previous marriage or marriages? What arrangements have been made for child support, if applicable, or succession upon your death?

        f.) When would you like to retire and what type of lifestyle do you want at that time?

    3.) Planners should make their questions as open-ended as possible to facilitate a dialogue.

ANALYZE AND APPLY

Nathaniel is meeting with his financial planner, Matthew, to identify his financial goals and objectives. Which of the following is(are) likely to take place as Matthew helps Nathaniel describe and list his goals and expectations?

1. Matthew encourages Nathaniel to prioritize his goals
2. Matthew tells Nathaniel what his other clients chose as financial goals
3. Matthew asks Nathaniel questions regarding the lifestyle he would like during retirement
4. Matthew makes recommendations regarding how Nathaniel can implement all of his goals

A. 1 only
B. 1 and 3
C. 2 and 4
D. 1, 2, and 3

Answer: B. As Nathaniel defines his goals and expectations, Matthew may ask Nathaniel questions regarding any career changes, business succession, or retirement lifestyle. Additionally, Matthew may encourage Nathaniel to prioritize multiple goals as his financial resources may not be sufficient to fund them all. This is not the time for Matthew to make specific recommendations; Nathaniel has not yet finalized his goals. Matthew should not tell Nathaniel what other clients selected as financial goals. Nathaniel's goals should be based on his specific circumstances. (Domain 2 – Gathering Information Necessary to Fulfill the Engagement)

c. Assess client's values, attitudes, expectations, and experience with financial matters – the planner should not allow his own values, attitudes, and expectations to influence his assessment of those of the client

d. Determine client's life cycle phase

    1.) As people progress through their life cycles, there is a tendency to move subtly among financial objectives as the result of changes in personal financial circumstances. These phases are known as:

        a.) Asset accumulation

        b.) Conservation/protection

        c.) Distribution/gifting

    2.) Financial planners can gain valuable insight into their clients' objectives and concerns by identifying which phases their clients are in at a given time. Goals within the life cycle are influenced by the following.

        a.) Age—A 35-year-old client may have saving for retirement and providing income to his family should he die as goals, while a 65-year-old's goals would more likely be having retirement income and using life insurance to leave an inheritance to his children and grandchildren.

        b.) Marital status and dependents—If married, mutual objectives should be considered. Children and parents dependent on the client will also influence goals (e.g., providing life insurance funds at the client's death and saving for the care of elderly parents).

        c.) Financial status—Level of income and net worth will affect goals (e.g., tax savings strategies for higher net worth clients)

        d.) Special needs—Special needs may result from, but not limited to, disabled dependents, nontraditional relationships, and children from previous marriages.

        e.) Attitudes, values, beliefs, biases, and behavioral characteristics—Clients may have varying perspectives regarding financial matters, such as retirement or leaving a legacy.

EXHIBIT 1: Life Cycle Phases and Characteristics

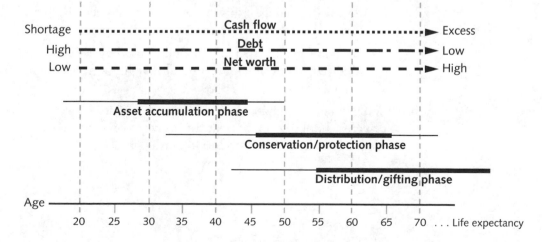

3.) Asset accumulation phase

a.) Begins between ages 20 and 25 and lasts until approximately age 45 or later if the client's children are not yet independent. The beginning of this phase is characterized by the following:

- Limited excess funds for investing
- High degree of debt to net worth
- Low net worth
- Lack of concern for risks

b.) As the person moves through the asset accumulation phase there is:

- An increase in cash for investments
- Less use of debt as a percentage of total assets
- An increase in net worth

4.) Conservation/protection phase

a.) A person is usually in this phase from approximately 45 to 60 or immediately preceding the client's planned retirement date

- May last throughout the client's working life or, in some cases, until death
- Also characterized by an increase in cash flow, assets, and net worth and typically some decrease in the proportionate use of debt

b.) People generally become more risk averse as more assets are acquired. Thus, they:

- are more concerned about losing what they have acquired than acquiring more; and
- become aware of and are concerned with many risks they ignored at the beginning of the asset accumulation phase, including an increased awareness of life's risks (e.g., untimely death, unemployment, or disability).

5.) Distribution/gifting phase

a.) Begins when a person realizes that he can afford to spend on things he may have never believed possible

- At the beginning of this phase a person may remain in both the asset accumulation and conservation/protection phases
- For many people, there is a period when they are being influenced by all three phases simultaneously, although not necessarily to the same degree

b.) When clients purchase new cars for adult children, pay for a grandchild's private school tuition, or treat themselves to expensive vacations, they are likely to be in the distribution/gifting phase

e.   Determine client's risk tolerance and risk exposure

   1.)   Risk tolerance: investor's willingness to accept risk (e.g., declines in the value of his investments)

      a.)   During risk assessment, risk tolerance may be considered as the tradeoff that clients are willing to make between potential risks and rewards

   2.)   The financial planner must know the client's risk tolerance levels to help determine the types of investments and the style of risk management best suited for the client

   3.)   The planner can help the client develop the right mix (based on the client's circumstances and risk tolerance)

      a.)   Between low premiums and high deductibles/low coverage or higher premiums with greater coverage (for insurance considerations)

      b.)   To determine the appropriate investment portfolio

   4.)   Risk tolerance levels are subject to misinterpretation because they are subjective. The statement, "I am not very risky," may mean something different to each client. Therefore, additional questioning using open-ended questions is needed to ensure understanding. The planner should also ask about the client's past actions during the market phases as an indication of his historical risk tolerance.

   5.)   Risk perception – the client's assessment of the magnitude of the risks being traded off

   6.)   Risk capacity – the degree to which a client's financial resources can cushion risks

   7.)   Loss aversion – this theory involves clients valuing gains and losses differently and as a result making decisions based on perceived gains rather than perceived losses

f.   Collect applicable client records and documents including financial statements, tax and investment statements, insurance policies, education plan information, retirement and employee benefit details, estate planning documents, and business documents

4.   Step 3: Analyzing and evaluating the client's current financial status (*Domain 3*)

a.   General financial status – assets, liabilities, cash flow, budgeting, and debt management

b.   Risk management and insurance evaluation – current insurance coverage, retained risks, asset protection, and client liquidity

c.   Government and employee benefits – availability, participation, and coverage levels

d.   Investment evaluation – asset allocation, investment strategies, types of investments

e.   Tax evaluation – income, estate, and gift tax issues; current tax strategies; tax compliance status

f.   Retirement evaluation – current retirement plans and strategies, accumulation and distribution planning

g. Estate planning evaluation – documents, estate tax liabilities, asset ownership, beneficiary designations, gifting strategies

h. Business ownership – business form, employer benefits, succession planning and exit strategy, risk management

i. Education planning evaluation – sources of financing, tax considerations

j. Special needs – divorce/remarriage considerations, nontraditional family planning, charitable planning, dependent adult needs, disabled child needs, and terminal illness planning

---

ANALYZE AND APPLY

Dave, a CFP® professional, is meeting with his client, Blakely, to review her financial plan. Blakely is a single mother with a three-year-old daughter. Due to cutbacks, Blakely has learned that she will be laid off in 90 days. She is concerned about having enough resources to provide for her during any period of unemployment. Which of the following statements is CORRECT?

1. Dave should have her contact her employer to review any COBRA coverage that may be available.
2. Dave should have her prepare a budget to analyze her immediate cash flow needs.
3. Dave should offer to loan her money, if needed temporarily, at market interest rates with a reasonable payback period.
4. After her layoff, Dave should have her apply for a home equity line of credit for emergencies.
A. 1 and 2
B. 2 and 4
C. 1, 3, and 4
D. 1, 2, 3, and 4

Answer: A. Statements 1 and 2 are correct. Blakely should contact her employer to review any COBRA benefits that may be available. Also, with Dave's assistance, she should complete a budget to analyze her cash flow needs during any period of unemployment. They may wish to review her assets to reveal any other sources of cash that could be used temporarily. Under Rule 3.7, a certificant shall not lend money to a client. Exceptions to this rule include: the client is a member of the certificant's immediate family, or the certificant is an employee of an institution in the business of lending money and the money loaned is that of the institution, not the certificant. Neither of these exceptions applies in this case. If warranted, a person should apply for a HELOC before a layoff. Banks will generally not approve a HELOC when a person is unemployed. (Domain 3 – Analyzing and Evaluating the Client's Current Financial Status)

5. Step 4: Developing and communicating the recommendation(s) (*Domains 4 and 5*)

a. Creating client-specific recommendations tailored to meet the goals and objectives of the client, in line with client's values, temperament, and risk tolerance

1.) Synthesize (incorporate) all findings from the analysis of the client's financial status into the recommendations.

2.) Consider alternatives. In many cases, there may be more than one method in which to achieve the client's goals, and alternate approaches should be presented. Advantages and disadvantages of each approach should be clearly identified to the client.

3.) May involve input from a team of advisors (e.g., accountant, trust officer, and estate planning attorney). The financial plan should explain the specific responsibilities of the planner, the client, and any other advisors involved in implementing the plan.

4.) Be mindful of the interrelationships of the financial planning recommendations.

5.) A comprehensive plan should have detailed recommendations that are well-documented.

b. Collaborating with the client to ensure that the plan meets the goals and objectives of the client, revising the plan as needed

c. Communicating the recommendations to the client

1.) Present a financial plan to the client reviewing:

a.) Client goals

b.) Assumptions

c.) Observations and findings

d.) Alternatives

e.) Recommendations

2.) When communicating the recommendations, use and understand the following:

a.) Emotional intelligence: includes the ability to recognize emotional expressions in oneself and the client, as well as selecting socially appropriate responses to both the circumstances and the client's emotions

b.) Active listening: paying full attention to what the client is saying and responding by paraphrasing the client's comments

c.) Leading responses: guide the client to give more detail, making a "meeting of the minds" more likely

d.) Body language: nonverbal messages involving facial expressions, gestures, and body posture

■ The tone, inflection, and quality of one's voice more greatly influence the message conveyed than do the words actually spoken.

■ Impacts how clients receive messages more than any type of communication.

e.) Context: a client's past history or conditions

■ Examples include attitudes, values, biases, behaviors, cultural influences, risk tolerance levels, and experience in financial matters

3.) Once feedback is obtained, revise recommendations as appropriate

4.) Provide documentation of recommendations and any applicable disclosures to client

5.) Confirm client's acceptance of recommendations

6. Step 5: Implementing the recommendation(s) (*Domain 6*)

  a. Create a prioritized implementation plan with timeline

  b. Assign responsibilities among the CFP® professional, the client, and any other professionals (e.g., accountants, attorneys, real estate agents, investment advisers, stockbrokers, and insurance agents)

  c. Support the client directly or indirectly with the implementation of the recommendation(s)

  d. Coordinate and share information, as authorized, with others

  e. Determine monitoring responsibilities with the client (e.g., what will be monitored, how often, communication methods)

ANALYZE AND APPLY

Grace is a wealthy client of Tom, a CFP® professional. She works with Tom to invest her retirement assets. Last year, Tom advised Grace that she was required to take an annual required minimum distribution (RMD) from her IRA. Since then, Grace has always calculated her annual RMD, although Tom has offered to perform this task. She does, however, want Tom to check her calculations when she completes them. Last year, Grace was traveling the entire month of December and did not take the appropriate RMD. She is upset and feels Tom has violated professional conduct standards for not calculating the RMD in her absence. She believes Tom should reimburse her $10,000, the amount of the excise penalty for not taking the distribution. What should Tom do?

A. File a claim on his errors and omissions insurance for $10,000.

B. Sign a promissory note and agree to pay Grace $1,000 per year plus interest until the $10,000 has been repaid.

C. Transfer $10,000 from his business account to Grace's bank account as it was his responsibility as a planner to see that the RMD was taken.

D. Inform Grace that it is her responsibility to assure appropriate RMDs are taken, and he would have been glad to assist if she had advised him she would not be doing the calculation this year.

Answer: D. Ultimately, the client has the responsibility to assure compliance with the required minimum distribution rules. There is no mention of an agreement between Grace and Tom in which he was to calculate the RMD. Because Tom was not liable, there is no reason for him to arrange for any type of payment to Grace. Tom filing a claim with his errors and omissions insurance company due to the error made by Grace would be unethical.

(Domain 6 – Implementing the Recommendations)

7. Step 6: Monitoring the recommendation(s) (*Domain 7*)

   a. Discuss and evaluate changes in client's personal circumstances (e.g., birth/death, age, illness, divorce, and retirement)

   b. Review performance and progress of the plan

   c. Review and assess changes in the legal, tax, and economic environments

   d. Make new recommendations to take into consideration changed circumstances

   e. Review the scope of work and redefine the client-planner engagement as appropriate

   f. Provide client ongoing support

ANALYZE AND APPLY

Brian, a CFP® professional, is meeting with his new client, Rebecca. He begins the meeting by inviting her to his conference room and providing her with refreshments. He starts the conversation by asking a multitude of open-ended questions designed to give him a better understanding of her personal and financial situation. Rebecca appears to be fidgeting, avoiding eye contact, and repeating his questions back to him for clarity. Brian determines that something is causing her to be distracted. He asks a few more questions, but she only provides him with short, unclear answers. How should Brian proceed with the meeting?

A. Based on her behavior, he should disengage from the relationship because there appears to be a lack of mutual understanding.

B. Ask her additional open-ended questions to continue the discussion toward the goal of selling her a financial plan.

C. Reschedule the appointment and provide her with his firm's disclosures and risk-profile questionnaire for her to complete prior to the next meeting.

D. Show Rebecca empathy by asking a few additional questions, but offer to reschedule the meeting for another time if she continues to be uncomfortable.

Answer: D. At this point, Brian has come to the conclusion that something is preoccupying Rebecca's mind. He may wish to continue to ask a few more questions to discover any personal issues that may be creating her uneasiness before proceeding with the interview. If she is still reluctant, he should reschedule the meeting for a more productive time. He should not press her by providing his firm's information or attempt to convince her to proceed with a financial plan. (Domain 1 – Establishing and Defining the Client-Planner Relationship)

II. FINANCIAL STATEMENTS

CFP Board Principal Knowledge Topic B.9.

A. PERSONAL FINANCIAL STATEMENTS

1. Personal statement of financial position

   a. Also known as a *personal balance sheet* or *net worth statement*

   b. Assets and liabilities should be presented at fair market value (FMV)

   c. Provides a "snapshot" of net worth *on a given date* (e.g., "As of December 31, 20XX")

   d. Formula to memorize: assets – liabilities = net worth

   e. Footnotes should be used to describe details of both assets and liabilities

      1.) Pay careful attention to footnotes, as information needed to answer exam questions is often found in the footnotes.

   f. Property should be identified by ownership (e.g., JT for joint tenants with rights of survivorship)

   g. Categories of assets—depends on type and use of asset

      1.) Three categories:

         a.) Cash and cash equivalents—maturities of less than one year

         b.) Investments (invested assets)

         c.) Personal use assets (e.g., residence, furniture, and autos)

      2.) Assets should be listed in order of liquidity (ability to convert to cash quickly), from most liquid to least liquid

   h. Liabilities should be categorized according to maturity date

      1.) Current liabilities—due in less than one year

      2.) Long-term liabilities—due in one year or more

i.   Classifications

Assets	Liabilities
Cash and cash equivalents	Mortgage loans
Cash	Auto loans
Checking & savings account balances	Education loans
Money market accounts	Credit card debt
CDs w/maturities < 1 year	
Assets expected to be converted to cash within 1 year	
Invested assets	
Stocks	
Bonds	
Mutual funds	
Retirement plans	
Assets w/maturities ≥ 1 year	
Personal use assets	
Residence	
Furniture	
Automobiles	Net worth (assets less liabilities)

EXHIBIT 2: Statement of Financial Position

Alex and Megan Smith

Statement of Financial Position

As of December 31, 20XX

ASSETS[1]			LIABILITIES AND NET WORTH[2]		
Cash/Cash Equivalents			**Liabilities**		
JT	Cash (money market)	$40,000	Current:		
			A	Credit card 1	$5,000
	Total cash/cash equivalents	$40,000	M	Credit card 2	7,000
			M	Credit card 3	8,000
Invested Assets			A	Auto 1 note balance	5,000
M	Publications, Inc.	$300,000	M	Auto 2 note balance	5,000
M	Megan's bakery	100,000		Current liabilities	$30,000
M	Megan's investment portfolio	90,000			
A	Single Premium Deferred Annuity	110,000	Long-Term:		
A	Alex's investment portfolio (IRA)	200,000	Mortgage—primary residence		$150,000
A	Defined benefit plan (vested)	400,000	Mortgage—vacation home		120,000
	Total invested assetss	$1,200,000		Long-term liabilities	$270,000
Personal Use Assets			**Total liabilities**		$300,000
JT	Primary residence	$300,000			
JT	Vacation home	180,000	**Net Worth**		$1,562,000
JT	Personal property and furniture	100,000			
A	Auto 1	20,000			
M	Auto 2	22,000			
	Total personal use assets	$622,000			
	Total Assets	$1,862,000	**Total Liabilities and Net Worth**		$1,862,000

Notes to financial statements:*

[1] All assets are stated at fair market value.

[2] Liabilities are stated at principal only.

Titles and Ownership Information

A = Alex

M = Megan

JT = joint tenants with right of survivorship—JTWROS

*Always pay special attention to the footnotes that appear on any financial statement.

ANALYZE AND APPLY

Richard has a current net worth of $100,000. He is considering the following transactions:

■ Taking out a home equity loan of $12,000 to pay for a trip to Europe

■ Paying off his auto loan of $4,000 using funds from his money market deposit account

■ Purchasing his deceased uncle's toy car collection for $2,000 with savings account funds, even though the toy cars are of no economic value

What would Richard's net worth be after these transactions?

A. $86,000
B. $84,000
C. $90,000
D. $88,000

Answer: A. Richard's $12,000 home equity loan for travel increases his liabilities and does not affect his assets. Payment of his auto loan will reduce debt by $4,000. However, the use of his money market deposit account to pay off the debt will reduce assets by $4,000. The net effect of this transaction on his net worth is $0. Purchasing his uncle's toy car collection for $2,000 with funds from his savings account decreases his assets by $2,000 as the toy cars are worthless. Therefore, his net worth decreases to $86,000 ($100,000 – $12,000 – $2,000). (Domain 3 – Analyzing and Evaluating the Client's Current Financial Status)

2. Personal statement of cash flows

   a. May be referred to as the *cash flow statement*

   b. Indicates a *period covered* (e.g., "January 1, 20XX, to December 31, 20XX" or "For the Year Ending December 31, 20XX"), contrasted to the personal statement of financial position, which provides values *as of a given date*

   c. Inflows – outflows (fixed, variable, and taxes) = net cash flow (or savings level)

   d. Inflows

      1.) Gross salaries

      2.) Interest and dividend income, regardless of whether reinvested

      3.) Gross rental income

      4.) Tax refunds due

      5.) Realized capital gains

      6.) Alimony or child support received

      7.) Trust income

      8.) Inheritances

      9.) Gifts

    e. Outflows

        1.) Savings and investment—by item

        2.) Fixed outflows—nondiscretionary (e.g., mortgage payments and auto loan payments)

        3.) Fixed outflows—discretionary (e.g., club dues and cable TV fees)

        4.) Variable outflows—nondiscretionary (e.g., food and medical expenses)

        5.) Variable outflows—discretionary (e.g., vacations and entertainment)

    f. Footnotes should be used to explain details of income and expenses, if necessary

EXHIBIT 3:   Statement of Cash Flows

Nicholas and Ashley Jones

Statement of Cash Flows

For the period January 1, 20XX, to December 31, 20XX

Inflows		
Nicholas's self-employment income	$42,000	
Ashley's salary	55,000	
Dividend income	1,220	
Interest income	1,110	
		$99,330
Outflows – Savings/Investments		
IRA contributions	$4,000	
Dividends reinvested	1,220	
Interest reinvested	1,110	
		$6,330
Fixed Outflows		
Mortgage (P&I)	$11,592	
Property taxes	3,000	
Homeowners insurance	720	
Telephone	1,200	
Auto (P&I) payment	9,000	
Auto insurance	1,800	
Gas/oil/maintenance	3,600	
Credit card payments	7,200	
		$38,112
Variable Outflows		
Food	8,490	
Utilities	1,200	
Medical/dental	2,400	
Clothing/personal care	3,600	
Child care	3,000	
Entertainment/vacation	3,000	
		$21,690
Taxes		
Federal income tax (W/H) – Ashley	$12,100	
FICA – Ashley	3,108	
Total self-employment tax – Nicholas	5,159	
Estimated payments – Nicholas	5,775	
Total taxes		$26,142
		$92,274
Net Cash Flow*		$7,056

*Difference between cash inflows and outflows; also known as savings level.

B. ANALYSIS OF FINANCIAL STATEMENTS

1. Planners should distinguish between the information reported on the statement of financial position versus the statement of cash flows. Equally important is the ability to identify how various client transactions affect each or both of these financial statements.

2. Ratio analysis: starting point when analyzing a client's financial situation

   a. Current ratio = current assets ÷ current liabilities

      1.) Indicates the ability to meet short-term obligations

      2.) Examines the relationship between the current assets and current liabilities

         a.) Current assets: can be converted into cash within one year

         b.) Current liabilities: due within one year

      3.) A higher current ratio is preferable; a ratio of greater than 1.0 indicates that the client can pay off existing, short-term liabilities with readily available, liquid assets. Appropriate target should be 1.0 to 2.0.

      4.) Current assets consist of cash, cash equivalents (e.g., money markets and CDs with one year or less to maturity), accounts receivable, and inventory (for businesses)

      5.) Current liabilities consist of accounts payable, current debts (e.g., annual amounts due on credit cards, home mortgages, or auto/boat loans), and taxes

---

ANALYZE AND APPLY

Robert owns the following assets:

Asset	Value
Cash	$1,000
Section 401(k) plan	$20,000
Bond maturing in 5 years	$10,000
Checking account	$7,500
CD maturing in 18 months	$2,500
Automobile	$20,000
Money market deposit account	$10,000

He also has credit card debt of $7,200 payable during the next 12 months and has signed a $5,000 note payable in full in 18 months. His mortgage payments due over the next year total $17,000. Based on the information provided, what is Robert's current ratio?

A. 0.6336

B. 0.7645

C. 1.5900

D. 1.6942

Answer: B. Classify the items listed above:

Asset	Value	Category
Cash	$1,000	Current asset
Section 401(k) plan	$20,000	Invested asset
Bond maturing in 5 years	$10,000	Invested asset
Checking account	$7,500	Current asset
CD maturing in 18 months	$2,500	Invested asset
Automobile	$20,000	Personal use asset
Money market deposit account	$10,000	Current asset
Credit card debt payable during next 12 months	$7,200	Current liability
Note payable in 18 months	$5,000	Long-term liability
Mortgage payments payable during next 12 months	$17,000	Current liability

Total value of current assets: $18,500

Total value of current liabilities: $24,200

Current ratio: 0.7645 ($18,500 ÷ $24,200)

(Domain 3 – Analyzing and Evaluating the Client's Current Financial Status)

b. Consumer debt ratio = non-housing monthly debt payments ÷ monthly net income

   1.) Ratio should not exceed 20%

   2.) Monthly net income: monthly gross income less monthly taxes

c. Housing ratios

   1.) Housing cost ratio = all monthly nondiscretionary housing costs ÷ monthly gross income ≤ 28%

      a.) All monthly nondiscretionary housing costs include principal, interest, taxes, insurance, and any condominium or neighborhood association fees (if a renter, then the ratio is rent + insurance ÷ monthly gross income ≤ 28%)

   2.) Debt-to-income ratio (total debt ratio) = all monthly debt payments and housing costs from above ÷ gross monthly income ≤ 36%

      a.) Monthly debt payments include, but are not limited to, payments for automobile loans, credit card debt, and student loans.

   3.) The 28% and 36% thresholds are common mortgage lender standards and are appropriate targets for most clients

Martin, a CFP® professional, has been providing Benjamin and Abby Barnett financial planning services for the past five years. Six months ago, the Barnetts discussed with Martin a possible purchase of a larger new home on five acres in a neighboring community. At that time, Martin calculated the Barnetts' housing cost and debt-to-income ratios, and they met the common lender standards. At that time, Martin recommended the Barnetts purchase the new home. The couple is meeting with Martin again today and advises him they have decided to apply for a mortgage on the new home next week. Because they meet lender standards, based on Martin's previous calculations, they are confident they will qualify for the mortgage. One of the reasons they need a new home, they say, is to garage the $200,000 motor home they purchased last month. What is the most appropriate action Martin should take next?

A. Refer Benjamin and Abby to a mortgage broker
B. Discuss the additional expenses involved in owning a larger house
C. Get specific information about the new house so Martin can recommend suitable homeowners insurance
D. Recalculate the Barnetts' debt-to-income ratio

Answer: D. Because the Barnetts may have acquired considerable debt when they purchased the motor home, Martin should recalculate the couple's debt-to-income ratio, taking into consideration any increased debt payments due to the purchase, along with any other changes in income and debt over the past 6 months. The Barnetts' debt-to-income ratio may have risen above the lender's acceptable level of 36%. (Domain 7 – Monitoring the Recommendations)

    d. Savings ratio = savings per year ÷ gross income. The appropriate ratio will depend on the client's age and financial goals. Generally, for older individuals, this ratio should be higher.

3. The statement of cash flows should be analyzed using a month-to-month comparison, calculating each outflow as a percentage of total income

    a. Objective is to develop a predictive model for each expenditure (e.g., savings is 10% of gross income)

4. Emergency fund

    a. Helps the client withstand a sudden negative financial disruption of income or extraordinary expense

    b. Comprised of cash and cash equivalents

    c. Should generally be three to six months' worth of nondiscretionary cash flows to accommodate unemployment, loss of significant assets, or other unexpected major expenditures

        1.) Nondiscretionary expenses—those expenses that remain after a job loss (e.g., mortgage, car loans, credit card loans, and taxes)

      2.) Amounts

        a.) Three months is generally used when there are two working spouses or a second source of income

        b.) Six months is generally used when the client is single or married and only one of the spouses works

5. Areas of focus when determining strengths and weaknesses

   a. Savings (particularly for retirement)

   b. Investments given risk tolerance and goals

   c. Risk coverage (e.g., insurance)

   d. Net worth given client goals

   e. Emergency fund

   f. Estate planning documents (e.g., wills) and asset transfer plan

   g. Articulation of goals

   h. Cash flow management skills (including proper debt management)

   i. Employment status

III.   CASH FLOW MANAGEMENT

CFP Board Principal Knowledge Topic B.10.

A.   BUDGETING

1. Requires planning for the expected, the recurring, and the unexpected

2. Process of projecting, monitoring, adjusting, and controlling future income and expenditures

3. May be used to determine the wage replacement ratio for retirement capital needs analysis

4. Steps in preparing a budget

    a. Collect records for the last 12 months (e.g., bank statements, check registers, credit card statements)

    b. Track expenses by category and by month over the 12-month period to examine trends in expenses

    c. Calculate each category as a percent of overall gross income

    d. Pay special attention to discretionary expenses (e.g., entertainment). If the client is not saving the proper amount, the additional savings needed will most likely come from reducing these expenses.

    e. Project the budget for the next 12 months, using the last 12 months as a template and making the necessary adjustments. Account for any changes (e.g., client has purchased a new car and now has a car loan).

    f. The client should compare each month's actual expenses to the budget. In this way, the client can spot/correct excess spending early in the budget year.

ANALYZE AND APPLY

Carrie, age 28, is engaged to Frank, age 30. Their wedding date is 9 months from today. This is the first marriage for both of them and they do not have any children. They tell you their primary financial goal is saving for a down payment on a home. Frank's parents are willing to provide the couple, as a wedding gift, with up to $40,000 to help with the purchase of the home. The cost of the home is $180,000 and they have current savings of $25,000 earmarked for this goal. What should you do next?

A. Explain to Frank that a $40,000 gift from his parents would be subject to gift tax.

B. Help the couple prepare a budget to assist in determining an affordable monthly payment.

C. Provide the couple with the name of a mortgage broker to help them choose the best vehicle to finance the purchase.

D. Ask the couple how they are paying for their wedding.

Answer: B. The first step is to prepare a budget to determine how much they can afford to pay on a monthly basis for a mortgage. After preparing a budget, you could inquire about how they plan to pay for the wedding. You could offer to provide the name of a mortgage broker, but this should take place after reviewing their ability to afford the home. To avoid any gift tax, his parents could simply split the gift between them and divide the proceeds among Carrie and Frank. The annual exclusion for 2017 is $14,000 per individual; therefore, his parents could give them a total of $56,000 before incurring a taxable event. (Domain 3 – Analyzing and Evaluating the Client's Current Financial Status)

B. SAVING AND CONSUMPTION HABITS

1. Information regarding a client's saving and consumption habits helps the planner develop a successful strategic financial plan for the client

2. If the client does not have a history of saving money consistently, he should develop a strategy in which money is directed into savings before he receives a paycheck

3. Savings goals should be clearly defined in terms of time and quantity (e.g., "save $300 for an emergency fund each month")

4. Historical behavior is the best indicator of future behavior. Therefore, a good way to collect information regarding the client's saving and consumption habits is by asking the client about previous saving and consumption habits.

C. DISCRETIONARY VERSUS NONDISCRETIONARY EXPENSES

1. A *discretionary* expense is a recurring or nonrecurring expense for an item or service that is either nonessential or more expensive than necessary

   a. *Fixed* discretionary expenses may include the following

      1.) Club dues

      2.) Premium cable TV fees

      3.) Video game subscriptions

      4.) Smart phones

   b. *Variable* discretionary expenses may include the following

      1.) Vacations

      2.) Entertainment costs

      3.) Alcohol

      4.) Gambling

2. A *nondiscretionary* expense is a recurring or nonrecurring expense that is essential for an individual to maintain his life

   a. *Fixed* nondiscretionary expenses may include the following

      1.) Rent or mortgage payments

      2.) Auto and health insurance premiums

      3.) Loan repayments

   b. *Variable* nondiscretionary expenses may include the following

   1.) Utilities

   2.) Taxes

   3.) Food

   4.) Home or car repairs

3. Both discretionary expenses and nondiscretionary expenses must be considered when preparing a budget

   a. Discretionary expenses plus nondiscretionary expenses equals the individual's total budgeted expenses for the period

   b. Any excess of income over budgeted expenses can be used as a cushion for unforeseen expenses, while an excess of expenses over income will result in the consumption of assets (e.g., savings) or an increase in liabilities (e.g., credit card balance)

ANALYZE AND APPLY

Owen, a CFP® professional, meets with new client, Ava, who is prepared to, with Owen's help, prepare a budget. Ava brings to the meeting a list of her monthly nondiscretionary and discretionary expenses:

Nondiscretionary		Discretionary	
Utilities	$350	Health club dues	$75
Rent	$1,100	Entertainment	$150
Premium cable TV service	$200	Dining out	$200
Insurance premiums	$400	Tickets – sporting events	$150
Coffee shop lattes	$120	Smartphone service	$180
Food	$500		
Taxes	$450		

Assuming he has all of the other information needed to prepare an accurate budget, which of the following should Owen do next?

A. Track expenses by category and by month over the previous 12 months

B. Recommend Ava's discretionary expenses be reduced or eliminated altogether and invest the savings

C. Point out errors in Ava's list of nondiscretionary/discretionary expenses

D. Prepare a budget for Ava based on the information gathered

Answer: C. Owen should have noticed Ava did not correctly categorize her expenses. Although many clients believe premium cable TV service and coffee shop lattes are essential and nondiscretionary, they are actually discretionary expenses that can be reduced or eliminated altogether if needed to create a realistic budget. Once these classifications are correct, Owen can proceed with tracking Ava's expenses. (Domain 2 – Gathering Information Necessary to Fulfill the Engagement)

D.   OTHER SAVINGS STRATEGIES

1. Automatic payments to investment accounts are a great way to have money transferred to investment (or savings) accounts on a regular monthly basis

2. Section 401(k) plan contributions through automatic payroll deductions are a great way to accumulate money for retirement on a tax-deferred basis

3. Paying off outstanding credit card balances before implementing a savings plan can be a good strategy

---

ANALYZE AND APPLY

Trent, age 30, has come to you for advice regarding college planning for his two-year old son, Charles. He has presented you with the following information.

■ Current annual salary – $66,700

■ Traditional IRA – $12,563 (no contribution/fully invested in a U.S. Government Bond Fund)

■ Section 401(k) – $23,087 (10% contribution/2% match)

■ Monthly rent payment – $1,235

■ Credit card debt – $2,205 (14.9% fixed)

■ Car – lease, fully paid by employer

■ Checking account balance – $1,937

■ Long-term disability insurance – 60% of salary to age 65, 90-day elimination period (group)

■ Life insurance – 2x salary (group), $500,000 20-year term (individual)

After completing a budget with Trent, you have determined that he has $200 per month in surplus cash flow. He tells you excitedly that the full amount may be used to fund a college plan for Charles. Through a risk profile questionnaire, you determine he has a moderate to aggressive risk tolerance. Based on the information provided, what should Trent do first?

A. Pay off his credit card balance.

B. Set up a Section 529 plan, invested in an S&P 500 Index fund, for Charles.

C. Establish an emergency fund using a money market mutual fund.

D. Reposition the assets in the Traditional IRA to reflect his risk tolerance.

Answer: C. At this point, Trent should use his surplus cash flow to establish an emergency fund. He does not have access to immediate cash and, in case of disability; he does not have enough set aside to cover his elimination period. Even though he could take a loan from his Section 401(k) in case of emergencies, this is not the most prudent method to cover these risks. Paying off his credit card debt, repositioning his Traditional IRA, and establishing a college plan for Charles should take place after establishing the emergency fund. (Domain 3 – Analyzing and Evaluating the Client's Current Financial Status)

IV. FINANCING STRATEGIES

CFP Board Principal Knowledge Topic B.11.

CFP Board Principal Knowledge Topic B.16.

A. DEBT – GENERAL CONCEPTS AND PRINCIPLES

1. Debt is appropriate when matched properly with the economic life of the asset and the ability to repay

> **E X A M P L E**   The purchase of an automobile that is expected to be used for three years (36 months) has a maximum realistic economic life of five years (60 months). Therefore, the automobile should be financed over 36 months but certainly no longer than 60 months.

2. Debt analysis

   a. Debt should be analyzed in terms of its cost (acquisition fees, interest rate, prepayment penalties) and the estimated useful life of the asset

   1.) In general, clients should avoid using debt to finance a lifestyle they cannot afford

   2.) The planner should be able to discern this tendency by examining the client's financial statements (increasing credit card balances, increasing amounts of cash flow being used to make debt payments)

   b. If the client has high consumer debt balances, a debt management program needs to be formulated

   1.) Typically, priority is given to retire the debt with the highest interest rate (while maintaining minimum monthly payments on the other debts)

B. HOME MORTGAGES

1. Types

   a. Fixed

   1.) Level interest rate for the term of the loan

   2.) Fixed payment amortization schedule

   3.) The shorter the term, the higher the monthly payment, given the same interest rate

   b. Variable (adjustable rate)

   1.) Interest rate may change, typically on an annual basis, according to a specified benchmark. Monthly payments can change.

   2.) ARMs without caps can allow for negative amortization to occur, which means the mortgage balance may become greater than the value of the home

  c. FHA (Federal Housing Administration)

   1.) Guaranteed by the federal government

   2.) Very low initial down payment, and sometimes lower interest rate due to the federal government's guarantee of repayment

   3.) Mortgage insurance is required

    a.) Mortgage insurance is a policy that protects lenders against losses that result from defaults on home mortgages

    b.) FHA requirements include mortgage insurance primarily for borrowers making a down payment of less than 20%

  d. VA (Veterans Administration)

   1.) For veterans of the U.S. armed services only

   2.) No down payment required

   3.) No mortgage insurance required

   4.) Same federal guarantee of repayment as with FHA loans

  e. Interest only

   1.) Only interest on the mortgage is paid monthly

   2.) Keeps mortgage payment to a minimum

   3.) Owner hopes the fair market value of the home will increase so that the principal can be paid off by sales proceeds

   4.) Very risky

  f. Reverse

   1.) With most mortgages, the borrower makes payments to the lender; here the "reverse" takes place

   2.) Lender pays homeowner an income stream secured by equity in the home

   3.) Amount of payments based on the fair market value of the home and the age of the borrower

   4.) Borrowers must be age 62 or older

   5.) Homeowner retains title but incurs an increasing amount of debt with each payment received from the lender

   6.) Repayment of the outstanding mortgage is required if the homeowner dies, sells the home, a predetermined loan period comes to an end, or the owner no longer occupies the home (typically for a period of 6–12 months)

  g. Home equity loans/lines of credit (second mortgage)

   1.) Essentially second mortgages using the current equity in the homeowner's primary residence to provide money for home improvements or other purposes

   2.) Home equity loan: borrower receives a lump sum in the amount of the loan

   3.) Home equity line of credit (HELOC): borrower is given a set amount of credit from which to borrow

4.) Debt can be used for any purpose without affecting its deductibility for income tax purposes

5.) Qualifying home equity debt for which interest may be deducted is the lesser of

a.) $100,000 married filing jointly or single filer ($50,000 if the taxpayer files married filing separately), or

b.) the fair market value of the primary residence reduced by the amount of current acquisition indebtedness

2. Mortgage selection issues

a. Length of ownership

1.) If the length of ownership will be relatively short, an ARM may be most cost-effective

a.) This is because the initial interest rate on the ARM is typically less than a fixed rate

b.) However, rates on ARMs can reset annually, usually with a 2%/6% cap (2% maximum rate increase per year, 6% lifetime cap) and in the long run may be more expensive than a fixed rate mortgage

b. Cash flow

c. Risk tolerance

d. Clients who are considering an ARM because it is the only way they can qualify for the amount they want to borrow should be counseled by the planner

1.) Because the initial monthly mortgage payment is low (due to the initially low interest rate), less income will be required to qualify for an ARM than a fixed rate mortgage

2.) However, this is usually a poor plan and may eventually lead to nonpayment of the mortgage (as interest rates reset higher and the client cannot pay) and eventual loss of the home (foreclosure)

e. Clients can usually get a lower interest rate if they pay "points," a payment to the lender that is made at settlement. The planner should conduct a cost-benefit analysis of this option.

f. When comparing a 15-year to a 30-year fixed-rate mortgage, the interest rates will usually be about 0.5% different assuming the same down payment. The cash flows will differ depending on the interest rate and the size of the mortgage.

EXAMPLE

	Sales Price	Down Payment	Closing Costs Paid	Mortgage Amount	Term in Months	Interest Rate	P&I Payment
Fixed 30-Year	$180,000	$36,000	$5,760	$144,000	360	5.5%	$818
Fixed 15-Year	$180,000	$36,000	$5,760	$144,000	180	5.0%	$1,139
ARM 30-Year	$180,000	$36,000	$5,760	$144,000	360	3.0%	$607

3. Savings due to mortgage selection

   a. The savings is a result of (1) the 15-year mortgage causing earlier retirement of the principal indebtedness and (2) the slightly lower interest rate. However, many 30-year loans are selected simply as a necessity to meet lender qualification requirements. If no prepayment penalties exist, most of the savings can be achieved by paying a 30-year loan according to a 15-year amortization schedule.

EXAMPLE

	Number of Payments	Monthly Payment (rounded)	Total Payments	Loan Amount	Total Interest Paid
30-Year Fixed	360	$818	$294,480	$144,000	$150,480
15-Year Fixed	180	$1,139	$205,020	$144,000	$61,020
Savings			$89,460	$0	$89,460

The total interest paid is determined by multiplying the amount of the payment by the number of payments and then subtracting the principal borrowed.

4. Mortgage payments consist of four components: principal (P), interest (I), taxes (T), and insurance (I) (Acronym: PITI)

   a. Time value of money mortgage problems calculate principal and interest only

   b. Taxes and insurance must be added to principal and interest

---

ANALYZE AND APPLY

Robert, a CFP® professional, meets with his new clients, Brandon and Abby, who are seeking advice regarding their financial affairs. During his review of Brandon and Abby's financial documents, Robert finds that the couple's necessary living expenses exceed their current income, and that they have no plan for funding the college education of their 12-year old daughter, Shelby. Mortgage rates are at an all-time low and Brandon and Abby would like to refinance their current 30-year mortgage to a 15-year mortgage. If they do this, their payments will be higher than their current payment, but the idea of paying off the mortgage sooner is attractive to them. What should Robert recommend regarding the couple's mortgage?

A. Refinance to a 30-year fixed mortgage and begin a savings plan

B. Meet with their mortgage broker to begin the refinancing process

C. Continue with their current mortgage, as the higher interest is tax deductible

D. Refinance to a 15-year mortgage, which would reduce the amount of interest paid over the life of the loan

Answer: A. Brandon and Abby currently have a negative cash flow, and this situation must be addressed as soon as possible. They should reduce their payments as much as possible and establish a cash reserve. When completed, they can meet with Robert to discuss education planning for Shelby.
(Domain 4 – Developing the Recommendations)

C.   BUYING VERSUS RENTING A HOME

1. The effect on cash flow when buying a home

    a. Mortgage payments (principal and interest)

    b. Down payment, closing costs, mortgage insurance, property insurance and taxes, maintenance, and operating expenses are all costs associated with purchasing a home. Families often purchase more life insurance when they own a home, in the event one of the spouses dies.

    c. Upfront charges place a heavy burden on the homeowner

    d. Mortgage interest (within limits), property taxes, and possibly mortgage insurance are tax deductible expenses

    e. There are different types of mortgage payments to choose from (variable rate, fixed rate, or balloon payment) that can affect both short-term and long-term cash flow

2. The effect on cash flow when renting living quarters

    a. Cost is fixed in the short term, and there is no long-term commitment

    b. No property tax associated with renting

    c. Maintenance and repair costs are usually included in the rent payment

    d. Cost of insurance is substantially lower than for a homeowner

    e. Consider saving toward the purchase of a house

3. The following example compares and contrasts a sample renter's and homeowner's expenses

E X A M P L E Comparison of Expenses—Renting vs. Buying a Home			
Renters insurance premiums	$250	Homeowners insurance premiums	$750
Property taxes	$0	Property taxes	$2,000
Annual rent	$8,400	Mortgage principal and interest	$7,200
Home maintenance	$0	Home maintenance	$3,700

4. Renting a home is beneficial if clients will not be in the home for a long period (over three to five years). If occupancy will be longer, purchasing a home is likely to be advantageous. Two major advantages of home ownership are the tax deductions (e.g., mortgage interest and property taxes) and home equity.

V.   FUNCTION, PURPOSE, AND REGULATION OF FINANCIAL INSTITUTIONS

CFP Board Principal Knowledge Topic A.5.

A.   BANKS AND SIMILAR INSTITUTIONS

1. Several financial institutions offer various forms of checking and savings accounts including

   a. Commercial banks

   b. Savings and loan associations

   c. Mutual savings banks

2. Federal Deposit Insurance Corporation (FDIC) insurance

   a. Any person or entity can have FDIC insurance on a deposit. A depositor does not have to be a U.S. citizen or even a resident of the United States.

   b. The FDIC insures deposits in some, but not all, banks and savings associations

   c. Federal deposit insurance protects deposits that are payable in the United States. Deposits that are only payable overseas are not insured.

   d. Securities, mutual funds, and similar investments are not covered by FDIC insurance

      1.) Creditors (other than depositors) and shareholders of a failed bank or savings association are not protected by federal deposit insurance

      2.) Treasury securities (bills, notes, and bonds) purchased by an insured depository institution on a customer's behalf are not FDIC insured

   e. All types of deposits received by a qualifying financial institution are insured

      1.) For example, savings deposits, checking deposits, deposits in NOW accounts, and time deposits (including certificates of deposit, or CDs) are all FDIC-insured deposits

      2.) Cashier's checks, money orders, officer's checks, and outstanding drafts are also insured

      3.) Certified checks, letters of credit, and traveler's checks for which an insured depository institution is primarily liable are also insured when issued in exchange for money or its equivalent or for a charge against a deposit account

   f. Deposits in different qualified institutions are insured separately

      1.) If an institution has one or more branches, the main office and all branch offices are considered to be one institution

      2.) Thus, deposits at the main office and at branch offices of the same institution are added together when calculating coverage

      3.) Financial institutions owned by the same holding company but separately chartered are separately insured

   g. The FDIC presumes that funds are owned as shown on the deposit account records of the insured depository institution

h.   The maximum FDIC-insured amount of a depositor is $250,000

    1.)   Accrued interest is included when calculating insurance coverage

    2.)   Deposits maintained in different categories of legal ownership are separately insured. Accordingly, a depositor can have more than $250,000 of insurance coverage in a single institution if the funds are owned and deposited in different ownership categories.

    3.)   The most common categories of ownership are single (or individual) ownership, joint ownership, and trust accounts

    4.)   Separate insurance is also available for funds held for retirement and business purposes

        a.)   FDIC coverage for retirement accounts (e.g., IRAs) that an individual has on deposit at an FDIC-insured institution is $250,000

i.   Federal deposit insurance is not determined on a per-account basis

    1.)   A depositor cannot increase FDIC insurance coverage by dividing funds owned in the same ownership category among different accounts within the same institution

    2.)   The type of account (whether checking, savings, CD, outstanding official checks, or other form of deposit) has no bearing on the amount of insurance coverage

j.   Single ownership accounts

    1.)   A single (or individual) ownership account is an account owned by one person

        a.)   Single ownership accounts include accounts in the owner's name; accounts established for the benefit of the owner by agents, nominees, guardians, custodians, or conservators; and accounts established by a business that is a sole proprietorship

    2.)   All single ownership nonretirement accounts established by, or for the benefit of, the same person are added together

        a.)   Total is insured up to a maximum of $250,000

        b.)   Includes savings accounts, CDs, NOW accounts, checking accounts, and money market deposit accounts

    3.)   If an individual owns and deposits funds in his own name but then gives another person the right to withdraw funds from the account, the account will generally be insured as a joint ownership account

EXAMPLE

Depositor	Type of Deposit	Amount Deposited
A	Savings account	$125,000
A	CD	100,000
A	NOW account	125,000
A's restaurant (a sole proprietorship)	Checking account	75,000
Total deposited		$425,000
Maximum amount of insurance available		(250,000)
Uninsured amount		$175,000

4.) The Uniform Gift to Minors Act is a state law that allows an adult to make an irrevocable gift to a minor. Funds given to a minor under the Uniform Gift to Minors Act are held in the name of a custodian for the minor's benefit. The funds are added to any other single ownership accounts of the minor, and the total is insured up to a maximum of $250,000.

k. Joint accounts

   1.) A joint account is an account owned by two or more individuals

   2.) Joint accounts are insured separately from single ownership accounts if each of the following conditions are met:

   a.) All co-owners must be natural persons. Legal entities such as corporations or partnerships are not eligible for joint account deposit insurance coverage.

   b.) Each co-owner must have a right of withdrawal on the same basis as the other co-owner

   ■ If co-owners have different signature rights over the account, this is not considered a right of withdrawal on the same basis

   ■ If a co-owner's right to withdraw funds is limited to a specified dollar amount, the funds in the account will be allocated between the co-owners according to their withdrawal rights and insured as single ownership funds

   > **EXAMPLE** A husband and wife are co-owners of a checking account. If the husband can withdraw funds on his signature alone, but the wife can withdraw funds only on the signature of both co-owners, then this requirement has not been satisfied. The husband and wife do not have equal withdrawal rights.

   > **EXAMPLE** If $100,000 is deposited in the names of a father and daughter, but the daughter has the right to withdraw only up to $5,000 from the account, $5,000 is allocated to the daughter and the remainder is allocated to the father. The funds, as allocated, are then added to any other single ownership funds of the father or daughter, respectively.

   c.) Each co-owner must have personally signed a deposit account signature card

   ■ Requirement need not be satisfied if the account is a certificate of deposit or a deposit obligation evidenced by a negotiable instrument

   ■ Requirement need not be satisfied if the account is maintained by an agent, nominee, guardian, custodian, or conservator (but the deposit must in fact be jointly owned)

   3.) The interests of each individual in all joint accounts she owns at the same FDIC-insured depository institution are added together

   a.) Insured up to the $250,000 maximum

b.)   Each person's interest (or share) in a joint account is deemed equal unless otherwise stated on the deposit account records

---

EXAMPLE   Insurance for joint ownership accounts

Account	Owners	Balance
#1	A and B	$200,000
#2	B and A	25,000
#3	A, B, and C	150,000
#4	D and A	180,000

A's Ownership Interest	
Account #1 (A and B)	$100,000
Account #2 (B and A)	12,500
Account #3 (A, B, and C)	50,000
Account #4 (D and A)	90,000
Total deposited:	$252,500

A's ownership interest in the joint account category is limited to $252,500, so $2,500 is uninsured.

B's Ownership Interest	
Account #1 (A and B)	$100,000
Account #2 (B and A)	12,500
Account #3 (A, B, and C)	50,000
Total deposited:	$162,500

B's ownership interest in the joint account category is $162,500. That amount is less than the $250,000 maximum, so it is fully insured.

C's Ownership Interest	
Account #3 (A, B, and C)	$50,000
Total deposited:	$50,000

C's ownership interest in the joint account category is $50,000. That amount is less than the $250,000 maximum, so it is fully insured.

D's Ownership Interest	
Account #4 (D and A)	$90,000
Total deposited:	$90,000

D's ownership interest in the joint account category is $90,000. That amount is less than the $250,000 maximum, so it is fully insured.

4.)   Community property laws do not affect deposit insurance coverage. In states recognizing this form of ownership, an account in the sole name of one spouse will be insured as the single ownership account of that spouse. Separately, a qualifying joint account in the names of both spouses will be insured as a joint account.

5.) A deposit account held in two or more names that does not qualify for joint account deposit insurance coverage is treated as being owned by each named owner as an individual, corporation, partnership, or unincorporated association, as the case may be, according to each co-owner's actual ownership interest. As such, each owner's interest is added to any other single ownership accounts or, in the case of a corporation, partnership, or unincorporated association, to other accounts of such entity, and the total is insured up to $250,000.

l. Business accounts

1.) Funds deposited by a corporation, partnership, or unincorporated association are FDIC insured up to a maximum of $250,000

    a.) Funds deposited by a corporation, partnership, or unincorporated association are insured separately from the personal accounts of the stockholders, partners, or members

    b.) To qualify for this coverage, the entity must be engaged in an independent activity. *Independent activity* means that the entity is operated primarily for some purpose other than to increase deposit insurance.

2.) Funds owned by a business that is a sole proprietorship are treated as the individually owned funds of the person who is the sole proprietor. Consequently, funds deposited in the name of the sole proprietorship are added to any other single ownership accounts of the sole proprietor, and the total is insured to a maximum of $250,000.

m. Retirement accounts

1.) The total amount insured across all retirement accounts held at a single institution is limited to $250,000

2.) This is provided that the accounts are in bank investment products, not securities

n. Revocable trust accounts

1.) Include a living trust or a family trust

2.) Used for estate planning

3.) Generally, $250,000 of coverage is afforded per owner, per beneficiary (subject to specific limitations and requirements)

    a.) The $250,000 per beneficiary coverage applies only up to $1,250,000 of total coverage for any one person's revocable trust

    b.) If the assets in the trust are worth less than or equal to $1,250,000, the FDIC will assume that the life interest of each beneficiary is valued at $250,000

    c.) If the assets in the trust are worth more than $1,250,000 (and there are more than five named beneficiaries), the FDIC coverage is the greater of $1,250,000 million or the aggregate of all beneficiaries' proportional interests, limited to $250,000 per beneficiary

> **EXAMPLE**   Alex establishes a revocable trust with eight beneficiaries, each with a proportionate interest equal to $210,000. The total amount of FDIC insurance coverage is $1,680,000 ($210,000 × 8 beneficiaries).
>
> If the trust had eight beneficiaries, seven of which each have a proportionate interest equal to $100,000, and one of which has a proportionate interest equal to $600,000 then the amount of FDIC insurance coverage is equal to $1,250,000 [($100,000 × 7) + $250,000 max per beneficiary = $950,000 which is less than $1,250,000, so the trust will be covered for $1,250,000].

    o.   Irrevocable trust accounts

        1.)   An irrevocable trust itself will qualify for up to $250,000 in coverage for the combined interests of contingent beneficiaries

        2.)   Additional coverage up to $250,000 *per beneficiary* may apply based upon the actuarial value of trust benefits for each individual beneficiary

            a.)   Will not apply if the beneficiary's interest is a contingent interest

            b.)   Will not apply if the beneficiary's interest is subject to the possibility that the trustee may divert assets away from that beneficiary

B.   CREDIT UNIONS

1. Nonprofit financial institutions owned by members with a common association (e.g., fraternal organizations or employees of a company)

2. Earnings from loan interest and investments are allocated to members in the form of dividends

3. Employment-related credit unions typically make use of payroll deductions for deposits and loan repayments

4. Some may offer free term life insurance and credit life insurance up to certain limits

5. National Credit Union Share Insurance Fund (NCUSIF)

    a.   Backed by full faith and credit of U.S. government

    b.   Insures member accounts of all federal and most state-chartered credit unions up to $250,000

C.   BROKERAGE COMPANIES

1. Licensed financial institutions that specialize in the selling and buying of securities

2. Usually receive a commission for the advice and assistance they provide; commissions are based on the buy/sell orders they execute

3. Stock brokerage companies usually offer money market accounts in which clients may place money while waiting to make investments in other securities, such as stocks and bonds

D. INSURANCE COMPANIES

1. Provides protection for assets and income against various insurable risks through risk sharing and risk transfer

2. For the most part, regulated by states—goals:

    a. Keep insurers solvent

    b. Safeguard policyholders against substandard insurer practices

    c. Ensure that coverage is available to all individuals

    d. Maintain competition among companies

3. Federal regulation

    a. COBRA and HIPAA (continuation of health insurance coverage)

    b. Federal taxation of insurance based products (e.g., life insurance withdrawals, annuity payments, long-term care premiums)

E. MUTUAL FUND COMPANIES

1. A mutual fund company raises money by selling shares to the public and investing the money in a diversified portfolio of securities

    a. Investments are professionally managed

    b. Securities within the fund are purchased and sold at the discretion of the fund manager

    c. Investors are provided with a prospectus outlining the portfolio's investment objective, costs, and features

2. Mutual funds are also known as open-end investment companies and constantly issue and redeem shares according to investor direction

F. TRUST COMPANIES

1. Acts as a trustee, fiduciary, or agent for clients

2. Offers investment management and estate planning services

3. Administers trust funds and estates

4. Regulated by state law

VI. EDUCATION PLANNING

CFP Board Principal Knowledge Topic C.17.

CFP Board Principal Knowledge Topic C.18.

CFP Board Principal Knowledge Topic C.19.

CFP Board Principal Knowledge Topic C.20.

CFP Board Principal Knowledge Topic C.21.

A. INTRODUCTION

1. One of the most common financial planning goals of parents is to provide an education for their children

2. Over the past decades, college tuition has risen at a rate that is considerably higher than the general rate of inflation

B. NEEDS ANALYSIS

1. Before creating an education funding plan, individuals should first determine the estimated needs

2. Examples of needs

   a. Tuition and tuition-related expenses

   b. Books, school supplies, and equipment (e.g., calculator and computer)

   c. Lodging

   d. Meals

   e. Transportation

   f. Entertainment (school sporting events) and leisure (health club)

   g. Travel expenses

   h. Tutoring (if necessary)

   i. Extracurricular (fraternity/sorority dues)

   j. Clothing and attire

   k. Other considerations particular to the student or family

C. EDUCATION SAVINGS CALCULATION

See the Education Funding section in *Understanding Your Financial Calculator* published by Kaplan Financial Education

D. EDUCATION TAX CREDITS AND DEDUCTIONS

1. American Opportunity Tax Credit

   a. Equals 100% of the first $2,000 of qualified expenses paid in the tax year, plus 25% of the next $2,000

   b. The maximum credit allowed in a given year is $2,500 per student, if there are $4,000 of qualifying expenses

   c. Requirements

      1.) Available for qualified tuition, enrollment fees, related expenses and expenses for textbooks and other course materials incurred and paid in the first four years of postsecondary education for the taxpayer, spouse, or dependent. Note that room and board are excluded.

      2.) Student must be enrolled no less than half time to be eligible

      3.) In 2017, the credit is subject to a phaseout based on the taxpayer's adjusted gross income

         a.) Married filing jointly: $160,000–$180,000

         b.) All other taxpayers: $80,000–$90,000

   d. Up to 40% of the eligible AOTC credit is refundable, so even those who owe no tax can get up to $1,000 of the credit for each eligible student as cash back. For example, if a taxpayer owes no taxes and is eligible to take the maximum AOTC of $2,500, he will receive a tax refund of $1,000 (40% of $2,500).

2. Lifetime Learning Credit

   a. Benefits

      1.) The Lifetime Learning Credit provides annual per taxpayer reimbursement for qualified tuition and related expenses per family in the amount of $2,000 per year

      2.) The taxpayer must spend $10,000 annually on qualified expenses to qualify for the full credit; however, a partial credit can be obtained with lower levels of education expense

      3.) This credit is based on a 20% factor of the qualified expenses; in other words, to obtain the full $2,000 credit, there must be qualified education expenses of at least $10,000

   b. Requirements

      1.) This tax credit is available for tuition and enrollment fees for undergraduate, graduate, or professional degree programs

      2.) Does not require enrollment in a degree program, nor does it necessitate at least half-time enrollment

      3.) The Lifetime Learning Credit can be claimed for an unlimited number of years

      4.) In 2017, the credit is subject to a phaseout based on the taxpayer's adjusted gross income

         a.) Married filing jointly: $112,000–$132,000

         b.) All other taxpayers: $56,000–$66,000

    c.   Coordination of the American Opportunity Tax Credit and the Lifetime Learning Credit

        1.)   If two or more children in the same household incur qualified expenses in the same year, the parents may claim a:

            a.)   Lifetime Learning Credit for the family;

            b.)   American Opportunity Tax Credit for each child; or

            c.)   Lifetime Learning Credit for one child and an American Opportunity Tax Credit for the other.

        2.)   Only one credit is allowed per child per year; in other words, the American Opportunity Tax Credit and the Lifetime Learning Credit may not both be claimed in the same year for the same student

3. Employer's Educational Assistance Program

    a.   An employer can reimburse an employee's tuition (both graduate and undergraduate), enrollment fees, books, supplies, and equipment, and these benefits are excluded from the employee's income up to $5,250 per year

    b.   The employer or employee cannot, however, also claim an education credit (American Opportunity Tax or Lifetime Learning Credit) for the same expenses. If the employee has expenses greater than $5,250, the employee will be permitted to claim an education credit for the expenses over $5,250 (assuming the employee also meets the requirements for the education credits).

4. Deduction for student loan interest

    a.   Allowed to student (or parent if a PLUS loan) for interest paid on loans incurred solely to pay qualified higher education expenses at eligible educational institutions

    b.   Interest is deductible as an adjustment to reach AGI (an above-the-line deduction)

    c.   Maximum: $2,500 per year

    d.   2017 phaseout limits

        1.)   Single taxpayers: $65,000–$80,000 modified AGI

        2.)   Married filing jointly: $135,000–$165,000 modified AGI

    e.   Borrowers are allowed to deduct interest over the term of their loan obligation

E.   SECTION 529 PLANS (QUALIFIED TUITION PLANS)

1. Plan sponsors

    a.   States are allowed to enact qualified tuition programs (QTPs) in accordance with IRC Section 529

        1.)   Each state can use its own statutory language, but the plan must be in conformity with Section 529 to be an eligible plan

        2.)   Although state plans may differ, they must all contain the required provisions under IRC Section 529

    b. Eligible educational institutions can also create plans

        1.) An eligible educational institution is generally an accredited postsecondary educational institution

        2.) To be an eligible educational institution, the plan must receive a ruling of determination from the IRS

2. Types of Section 529 Plans (QTPs)

    a. Prepaid tuition plans

        1.) Allow contributors (usually parents) to prepay tuition today at a particular school for an individual in the future

        2.) The plan will lock in today's prices but subjects the participant to risks

            a.) The beneficiary may choose a school different from the one named in the plan

            b.) The beneficiary may not be accepted into the school named in the plan

        3.) Before investing in this type of plan, the participant will want to investigate the details of the particular plan as they relate to the previously listed factors

    b. College savings plan

        1.) This plan allows an individual to make contributions today into a savings fund

        2.) The earnings grow tax deferred

        3.) If the proceeds are used for higher education expenses, the distributions are tax free

3. Section 529 Plan (QTP) rules

    a. Contributions must be made in cash

        1.) Cash, check, money order, and credit cards are acceptable

        2.) A contribution of property is not allowed

    b. Plans must use separate accounting for each beneficiary

    c. Direction of investments

        1.) A college savings plan can permit the contributor to select among different investment strategies designed exclusively for the program when the initial contribution is made to establish the account

            a.) The investment options offered in college savings plans often include stock mutual funds, bond mutual funds, and money market mutual funds

            b.) Some plans offer age-based portfolios that automatically shift toward more conservative investments as the beneficiary gets closer to college age

    d. The account cannot be pledged as security for a loan

4. Plan advantages

    a. Tax-deferred growth

    b. Tax-free distributions if used for education

     c.   Generally, removes assets from estate

     d.   Generally, low commission and management fees

     e.   Many states offer state income tax deductions for contributions

     f.   The owner can change the beneficiary at any time

     g.   The owner decides when and how expenses are paid

     h.   The amount deposited varies by state but can be as much as is reasonable to fund education costs; most vary from $100,000 to $250,000

     i.   For gift tax purposes, contributions can be treated as though they were made ratably over a five-year period

     j.   Contributions are not phased out, even at higher AGI levels

     k.   Can be coordinated with other education plans but no double dipping is allowed (i.e., if the beneficiaries claim the Lifetime Learning Credit or American Opportunity Tax Credit, then no tax advantages are allowed for the same expenses)

5. Qualified expenses

     a.   Tuition

     b.   Fees

     c.   Books

     d.   Supplies

     e.   Certain room and board expenses (requires at least half-time status)

         1.)   Normally assessed fee, if school lodging

         2.)   School determines reasonable amount for other locations

6. Gift tax consequences

     a.   Contribution can be a split gift (e.g., half made by the donor and half by the donor's spouse)

     b.   Contribution is considered a completed gift of a present interest, therefore, qualifying for the annual exclusion

     c.   Favorable gift tax rules at contribution—five-year accelerating can be elected, allowing an individual to use five years' worth of annual exclusions on an initial contribution

> **EXAMPLE**   In year 1, when the annual exclusion is $13,000, Alan makes a contribution of $70,000 to a QTP for the benefit of his child, Stephen. Alan elects to account for the gift ratably over a five-year period beginning with the calendar year of contribution. Alan is treated as making an excludable gift of $13,000 in each of years 1 through 5 and a taxable gift of $5,000 in year 1.
>
> Assuming in year 3 the annual exclusion is increased to $14,000, Alan makes an additional contribution for Stephen's benefit in the amount of $7,000. Alan is treated as making an excludable gift of $1,000; the remaining $6,000 is a taxable gift in year 3.

     d.   See *Book 6 – Estate Planning* for more information on gift taxes.

7. Change of beneficiary

    a. Permitted at any time

    b. Rollovers will not be considered a taxable distribution if the funds are transferred to one of the following within 60 days of the distribution

        1.) To another qualified tuition program for the benefit of the designated beneficiary (provided a previous transfer to a qualified tuition program for the benefit of the designated beneficiary has not occurred within the last 12 months)

        2.) To the credit of another designated beneficiary under a qualified tuition program who is a member of the family of the designated beneficiary with respect to which the distribution was made

    c. Any change in the designated beneficiary of an interest in a qualified tuition program will not be a taxable distribution if the new beneficiary is a member of the previous beneficiary's family

    d. Gift tax consequences of a change of beneficiary

        1.) A transfer that occurs as a result of a change in the designated beneficiary, or a rollover of credits or account balances from the account of one beneficiary to the account of another beneficiary, will be treated as a taxable gift by the previous beneficiary to the new beneficiary if the new beneficiary is assigned to a lower generation than the previous beneficiary, whether or not the new beneficiary is a member of the previous beneficiary's family

> **EXAMPLE**   In year 1, a parent makes a contribution to a QTP on behalf of his child. In year 4, the parent directs that a distribution from the account for the benefit of the child be made to an account for the benefit of a grandchild. The rollover distribution is treated as a taxable gift by the child to the grandchild because the grandchild is assigned to a generation below the child.

8. Funds used for nonqualified expenses

    a. The earnings portion of the distribution is included in the gross income of the distributee

    b. A 10% additional tax will be applied to any distribution that is includable in gross income, on the basis of the previously listed rules

    c. The penalty is waived if the distribution is:

        1.) Made to a beneficiary (or to the estate of the designed beneficiary) on or after the death of the designated beneficiary

        2.) Made because the designed beneficiary is disabled

        3.) Made on account of a scholarship, allowance, or payment being received by the account holder to the extent that the amount of the payment or distribution does not exceed the amount of the scholarship, allowance, or payment

9. Distribution of funds

    a. Distributions are prorated between contributions and earnings

> **EXAMPLE** Assume the contributor deposited $4,500 and the account had earnings of $500 (total account value of $5,000). A nonqualified distribution of $200 is taken. In this case, 90% of the distribution is a tax-free return of basis, and 10% is earnings ($500/$5,000) subject to taxes. Therefore, $20 of the distribution (10% of $200) is taxable.

10. Limits to amounts contributed

   a. State sets limit

   b. Contributions cannot exceed reasonable cost of education

F. COVERDELL EDUCATION SAVINGS ACCOUNTS (CESAs)

1. Introduction

   a. Coverdell Education Savings Accounts (CESAs) are designed to offer tax benefits to individuals who wish to save money for a child's or grandchild's qualified education expenses

   b. A CESA is an investment account established with nondeductible contributions of cash

2. Benefits

   a. Contributions grow tax free

   b. Withdrawals are free from tax or penalty if the funds are used for qualified education expenses

   c. Qualified education expenses are not limited to higher education (undergraduate and graduate) but include such expenses for private elementary and secondary education (K-12)

   d. If the funds are used for anything other than qualified expenses, the earnings are generally subject to income tax and a 10% penalty

   e. Generally, the parent (responsible individual) maintains the right to change the beneficiary to another family member at any time

3. Requirements

   a. A CESA can be established for any child under age 18 by a parent, grandparent, other family members or friends, or even by the child, subject to modified adjusted gross income phaseouts.

   b. Contributions

      1.) Cannot be made after the beneficiary reaches age 18 unless he is a special needs beneficiary

      2.) Must be in cash

   c. Phaseout limits for 2017

      1.) Single taxpayers: $95,000–$110,000 modified AGI

      2.) Married filing jointly: $190,000–$220,000 modified AGI

    d. Annual contributions can be made up to $2,000 for each beneficiary. This includes contributions from all sources, including parents and grandparents.

    e. The definition of qualified education expenses for post-secondary school expenses include the following:

        1.) Tuition and mandatory fees at eligible educational institutions

            a.) For a school to qualify, it must be able to participate in federal financial aid programs administered by the Department of Education

        2.) Books, supplies, and computer equipment for courses

        3.) Room and board paid directly to the school if the student is enrolled at least half time

        4.) Expenses for special-needs services for special-needs students

    f. The definition of qualified education expenses for elementary and secondary school expenses includes the following:

        1.) Tuition, fees, academic tutoring, special need services, books, supplies, and other equipment incurred in connection with the enrollment or attendance of the beneficiary at a public, private, or religious school providing elementary or secondary education (kindergarten through grade 12) as determined under state law

        2.) Room and board, uniforms, transportation, and supplementary items or services (including extended day programs) required or provided by such a school in connection with such enrollment or attendance of the beneficiary

        3.) The purchase of any computer technology or equipment or Internet access and related services, if such technology, equipment, or services are to be used by the beneficiary and the beneficiary's family during any of the years the beneficiary is in school

    g. When the beneficiary attains age 30 (unless the beneficiary has special needs or dies), the account must be distributed to the beneficiary within 30 days. The distribution will be subject to income tax and the 10% penalty as discussed within this section.

        1.) The CESA may be rolled over (tax and penalty free) into a CESA for a family member of the original beneficiary. If the new beneficiary is a generation below the generation of the original beneficiary, the distribution is treated as a taxable gift.

        2.) If the beneficiary dies and the account has not been distributed during the 30-day period, the remaining balance is considered distributed to the beneficiary and included in the beneficiary's estate

4. Gift tax consequences

    a. Contribution can be a split gift (i.e., half made by the donor, and half by the donor's spouse)

    b. Contribution is considered a completed gift of a present interest, allowing it to qualify for the annual exclusion

5. Distributions and withdrawals

    a. Distributions or withdrawals from CESAs are composed of principal and earnings

    b. The designated beneficiary of a CESA may take withdrawals at any time; distributions are always paid to the beneficiary (or beneficiary's estate) and will not be repaid to the contributor

    c. The principal is always excluded from taxation, whereas earnings are excluded if they are used to pay for qualified education expenses

    d. Withdrawals are tax free whether the student is enrolled full time, half time, or less than half time as long as the withdrawals do not exceed the student's qualified education expenses

6. Penalty on certain distributions

    a. A 10% additional tax will be applied to any distribution that is includable in gross income, on the basis of the previously listed rules

    b. The penalty is waived if the distribution is:

        1.) Made to a beneficiary (or to the estate of the designated beneficiary) on or after the death of the designated beneficiary

        2.) Made because the designated beneficiary is disabled

        3.) To the extent that the beneficiary receives a tax-free scholarship

7. Coordination with tax credits

    a. A taxpayer can claim an American Opportunity Tax Credit or Lifetime Learning Credit for a taxable year and can exclude from gross income amounts distributed (both the contributions and the earnings portions) from a CESA on behalf of the same student, as long as the distribution is not used for the same education expenses for which a credit was claimed

ANALYZE AND APPLY

Grant, a CFP® professional, has been providing Matt and Hannah Taylor financial planning services for the past seven years. Today, they are meeting for an annual review of their financial plan. During this meeting, they discuss the education funding goals the Taylors have for their two children, Noah, age 18, and Emma, age 13. Noah graduated last month from Pinecrest Academy, a private school, and Emma will continue her education there when school resumes in two months. When Noah was young, the Taylors established a CESA for Noah's college expenses. They did not establish one for Emma because her great uncle funded a trust for her undergraduate college education shortly after she was born. Since Grant's last meeting with the Taylors, Noah has received a full 4-year scholarship from Marshall University (MU) covering all his expenses, including full-time tuition, room and board on campus, and books. He will enter MU later this month. In light of this change in circumstances, which of the following is the most appropriate action Grant should take?

A. Suggest that the Taylors discontinue making contributions to the CESA
B. Recommend the Taylors continue to contribute to the CESA while Noah is an undergraduate in anticipation of using the account to pay for his graduate school expenses
C. Advise the Taylors to withdraw funds from the CESA for any expenses associated with Noah living off campus in an apartment should he decide to do so while studying at MU
D. Propose the Taylors roll over Noah's CESA into a CESA for Emma and use the funds in the new account to cover Emma's Pinecrest Academy tuition, tutoring, and computer expenses for the next 5 years

Answer: D. The best course of action is for the Taylors to roll over Noah's CESA into a CESA for Emma. Under CESA rules, qualified expenses include expenses for elementary and secondary school education, so Emma's new CESA can be used for her current education expenses. This is a better choice than discontinuing contributions into Noah's CESA because there is no guarantee that he will need the funds for future education expenses. The Taylors cannot continue to contribute making contributions into Noah's CESA; contributions cannot be made after the beneficiary (Noah) reaches age 18. Although the Taylors can withdraw funds from Noah's CESA to pay for his off-campus living expenses, there will be a 10% additional tax on any earnings withdrawn from the fund. (Domain 7 – Monitoring the Recommendations)

G. SAVINGS BONDS

1. Series EE savings bonds (EE bonds)

    a. Under normal circumstances, the accumulated interest on Series EE and I bonds that are cashed in is taxable income. However, if the bonds are cashed in during a year in which the taxpayer or taxpayer's family member has qualified higher education expenses, this interest avoids taxation (within limits).

    b. Face values of EE bonds start as low as $25 and increase up to $10,000

    c. EE bonds are purchased electronically at full face value

    d. EE bonds have varying interest rates

    e. They must be purchased after 1989 to be eligible for special tax treatment

    f. Qualified higher education expenses include rolling over proceeds from the savings bonds into a qualified tuition program (IRC Section 529 Plan) or a CESA

    g. To attain tax-free status, EE bonds must be purchased in the name of one or both parents of the student/child

    h. The parent(s) are considered the owners of the bond and must be at least 24 years old before the first day of the month of the issue date of the bond

    i. Also, the owners must redeem the bonds in the same year that the student/child's qualified higher education expenses are paid

    j. The exclusion is subject to a phaseout in the years in which the bonds are cashed and the tuition is paid. The modified adjusted gross income phaseouts for 2017 are $117,250–$147,250 for joint returns and $78,150–$93,150 for other returns. Married taxpayers filing separately do not qualify for the exclusion.

    k. Series I bonds have the same tax benefits as EE bonds for purposes of qualified higher education expenses

H. GOVERNMENT GRANTS AND LOANS (FINANCIAL AID)

  1. Types of financial aid

    a. Federal Pell Grants

      1.) Outright gifts from the government based on the student's need and the cost of attending the chosen school

      2.) Only undergraduate students who have not previously received a bachelor's degree are eligible

      3.) The maximum award changes each year depending on program funding

      4.) Largest need-based student aid program

    b. Federal Supplemental Educational Opportunity Grant (SEOG) Program

      1.) Grant program for undergraduates with exceptional financial need

      2.) Managed by colleges instead of the federal government

      3.) Students are automatically considered when they submit a FAFSA form

    c. Federal Perkins Loan Program

      1.) Federally funded program administered by colleges

      2.) Provides loans of up to $5,500 per year for undergraduate students and $8,000 per year for graduate students, with cumulative limits of $27,500 for undergraduate loans and $60,000 for undergraduate and graduate loans combined

3.) Characteristics include a 5% fixed interest rate, deferred repayment, a nine-month grace period, and a maximum of 10 years to repay the loan. Students are automatically considered if they complete a FAFSA.

    a.) Interest is subsidized by the federal government while the student is in school and during the 9-month deferral period

d. Federal College Work-Study Program

1.) Sponsored by the government and administered through colleges

2.) Students work 10–15 hours per week at a job that is typically on campus, to earn a portion of their financial aid package

e. Federal PLUS Loans

1.) Allow the parents of undergraduate students to borrow up to the total cost of education less other financial aid awards

2.) Loans are not made on the basis of financial need, but borrowers must show that they do not have unsatisfactory credit history

3.) Repayment of the loan must begin within 60 days of disbursement

4.) Loans of graduate and independent undergraduate students are placed into deferment while students are enrolled at least half-time and for an additional six months after students cease to be enrolled at least half-time

f. Subsidized Federal Stafford Loans

1.) Based on financial need

2.) The government pays the interest while the student is enrolled in college

3.) Repayment of the loan may take up to 10 years and is deferred until six months after the student graduates, leaves school, or drops below half-time status

g. Unsubsidized Federal Stafford Loans

1.) Available for students who do not qualify for subsidized loans or require additional funds

2.) For unsubsidized loans, the government does not pay the interest during the college years; however, the interest may be capitalized. Repayment rules are the same as Subsidized Federal Stafford Loans (see previous section).

3.) Both types of Stafford loans are available to undergraduate and graduate students

2. Since the passage of the Health Care and Education Reconciliation Act of 2010, Stafford, PLUS, and Consolidation Loans have been made directly by the federal government through the Direct Loan program.

I.   OTHER SOURCES

1. Traditional IRA

    a. Generally speaking, if a taxpayer withdraws funds from a traditional IRA before age 59½, the taxpayer is required to pay a 10% early withdrawal penalty on all or part of the amount withdrawn

    b. The 10% penalty does not apply if a taxpayer withdraws funds from a traditional (or Roth) IRA to pay for qualified higher education expenses for the taxpayer, the taxpayer's spouse, or the child or grandchild of the taxpayer or taxpayer's spouse

    c. The taxpayer will owe federal income tax on the amount withdrawn

2. Roth IRA

    a. Contributions

        1.) The Roth IRA does not provide for tax-deductible contributions

        2.) Contributions grow tax free within the IRA

    b. Distributions

        1.) A distribution from a Roth IRA is not includable in the owner's gross income if it is a qualified distribution or to the extent that it is a return of the owner's contributions

        2.) Qualified distributions are those that occur after a five-year holding period and for one of the following four reasons

            a.) Death

            b.) Disability

            c.) Attainment of age 59½

            d.) First-time house purchase (limit of $10,000)

        3.) If a distribution is not a qualified distribution and it exceeds the contributions (and conversions) to Roth IRAs, the distribution will be subject to income tax and may be subject to the 10% penalty

        4.) Excess distributions can avoid the 10% penalty if the proceeds are used for qualified higher education costs

        5.) The taxpayer is always able to withdraw amounts up to the total contribution without income tax or penalty

    c. Benefits

        1.) Distributions used for qualified higher education expenses escape the 10% penalty, regardless of the family member's age

            a.) This compares favorably with CESAs, which are restricted to qualified use by age 30 unless the beneficiary has special needs

        2.) Funds not used for education can be used for retirement of the account owner

        3.) Qualified higher education expenses include:

            a.) Tuition

            b.) Fees

            c.) Room and board (only for students who are enrolled at least half-time)

3. Home equity borrowing

    a. A home equity loan or a home equity line of credit (HELOC) may be used to fund college-related expenses

    b. Because home equity loans are secured by a home, the interest rate on a home equity loan may be lower than rates for an unsecured student loan

    c. Many state schools do not consider the value of the home when determining eligibility for financial aid, but numerous private colleges take home equity into account

    d. If home equity is considered in the financial aid equation, a home equity loan could decrease home equity and possibly improve one's eligibility for financial aid

    e. Interest on home equity loans is normally deductible as an itemized deduction

    f. As a general rule, using home equity loans to pay for higher education expenses should be a last resort, or at least done after researching all other options, rates, and conditions for alternative funding

4. Uniform Gift to Minors Act/Uniform Transfers to Minors Act

    a. The Uniform Gift to Minors Act (UGMA) or Uniform Transfers to Minors Act (UTMA) allows parents the option to put assets in a custodial account for a child

    b. If the child is younger than age 19 (or age 24 if a full-time student), a portion of the child's unearned income (i.e., interest and dividends) may be taxed at the income tax rate of the parents

    c. Custodial account assets are considered an asset of the child and are considered in determining financial aid

5. Highlights of tax benefits for higher education

The following exhibit provides a glance at the highlights and attributes of the various vehicles covered in this section.

EXHIBIT 4:   Highlights of Tax Benefits for Higher Education for 2017

	American Opportunity Tax Credit	Lifetime Learning Credit	Coverdell Education Savings Account (CESA)[1,2]	Traditional, Roth, SEP, & SIMPLE IRAs[1]	Student Loan Interest	Qualified Tuition Programs[4] (Section 529 Plans)	Education Savings Bond Program[1]	Employer's Educational Assistance Program[1]
What is your benefit?	Credits can reduce the amount of tax you must pay	Earnings are not taxed	No 10% additional tax on early withdrawal	Interest is tax deductible	Earnings are not taxed	Interest is not taxed	Employer benefits are not taxed
What is the annual limit?	Up to $2,500 per student	Up to $2,000 per family	$2,000 contribution per beneficiary	Amount of qualifying expenses	$2,500	Determined by sponsor	Amount of qualifying expenses	$5,250
What expenses qualify besides tuition and required enrollment fees?	AOTC expands eligible expenses to include course materials, computers, and Internet access used for education	None	Books, supplies, & equipment Room and board if at least a half-time student Payments to state tuition program	Books, supplies, & equipment Room and board if at least a half-time student	Books, supplies, & equipment Room & board Transportation Other necessary expenses	Books, supplies, & equipment Room and board if at least a half-time student	Payments to CESAs Payments to qualified tuition program	Books, supplies, & equipment
What education qualifies?	First 4 years of undergraduate	All undergraduate and graduate[2]						
What are some of the other conditions that apply?	Can be claimed for 4 years Must be enrolled at least half-time in a degree program		Can also contribute to CESAs and qualified tuition programs in the same year Must withdraw assets at age 30 unless the beneficiary has special needs		Must have been at least half-time student in a degree program	Distribution is excluded from gross income. AOTC and Lifetime Learning Credit are permitted in the same year but not for the same expenses.	Applies only to qualified Series EE bonds issued after 1989 or Series I bonds	
In what income range do benefits phase out?	2017 Single $80,000–$90,000 MFJ $160,000–$180,000	2017 Single $56,000–$66,000 MFJ $112,000–$132,000	2017 Single $95,000–$110,000 MFJ $190,000–$220,000	No phaseout[3]	2017 Single $65,000–$80,000 MFJ $135,000–$165,000	No phaseout	2017 Single $78,150-$93,150 MFJ $117,250-$147,250	No phaseout

[1] Any nontaxable withdrawal is limited to an amount not exceeding qualifying education expenses.

[2] For CESAs, qualified elementary and secondary school expenses are also permitted.

[3] Phaseouts exist at time of contribution. They are not relevant for withdrawals.

[4] Exclusion is extended to distributions from Qualified Tuition programs established by an entity other than a State after December 31, 2003.

Molly, age 42, and Steven, age 50, have one child, Jennifer, age 17. The couple has been your client for 15 years. They have set up a review meeting with you to discuss funding their daughter's first year of college, which will begin in 6 months. They estimate qualified expenses of $35,000, of which $20,000 will be covered by an academic scholarship. Also, they have expressed a concern about any tax ramifications of their decision. The couple has a MAGI of $140,000 and itemized deductions of $24,000. The following information is contained on their current statement of financial position:

- Section 529 Plan - $57,987
- Series EE Savings Bonds (owned by Jennifer) - $10,000
- Variable universal life insurance cash value (Steven) - $26,453
- Roth IRA (Molly) - $5,000
- Section 401(k) (Molly and Steven combined) - $345,928

Which of the following should be utilized to fund Jennifer's first year of college expenses?

A. The scholarship and Section 529 Plan.
B. A combination of the Lifetime Learning Credit, American Opportunity Tax Credit, and a loan from one of their Section 401(k) plans.
C. The Series EE Savings Bonds and a distribution from the Roth IRA.
D. A loan from the variable universal life insurance cash value and a Pell Grant.

Answer: A. The couple should use the academic scholarship of $20,000 and a distribution of $15,000 from the Section 529 plan to fund Jennifer's first year of qualified college expenses. In order to qualify for favorable tax treatment, the Series EE Savings Bonds must be owned by a parent. Federal Pell Grants are outright gifts from the government based on the student's financial need and the cost of attending the chosen school. Based on their MAGI, they probably would not qualify for a Pell Grant. Also, taking a loan on the VUL policy would reduce any future cash value growth. Because they have a Section 529 plan, taking a loan and/or withdrawal from their retirement plans would not be a wise choice. (Domain 7 – Monitoring the Recommendations)

VII.   ECONOMIC CONCEPTS

CFP Board Principal Knowledge Topic B.12.

A.   DEMAND AND SUPPLY

1. Demand

    a. The amount of a commodity people buy depends on its price

    b. The relationship between price and quantity bought is called the demand curve

        1.) Downward sloping demand—if the price of a commodity is raised, all other things being equal, buyers tend to buy less

        2.) The demand curve measures price on the vertical axis and quantity demanded on the horizontal axis

EXHIBIT 5:   The Demand Curve

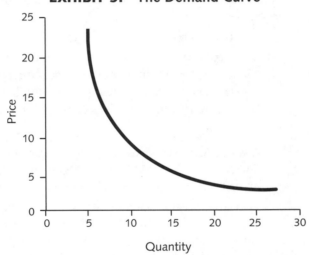

        3.) When the price is lowered, all other things being equal, quantity demanded increases

    c. Quantity demanded tends to fall as price rises for two reasons

        1.) Substitution effect—when the price of a good rises, consumers substitute other similar goods

        2.) Income effect—when the price rises, consumers curb consumption

    d. Factors affecting demand

        1.) The price of the good

        2.) The average income of consumers. As incomes rise, individuals tend to buy more.

        3.) Population

        4.) The prices and availability of related goods

        5.) Tastes and preferences

        6.) Special influences, such as expectations about future economic conditions, particularly prices

e. A "shift in demand" or a "change in demand" is different from "change in quantity demanded"

    1.) A "shift" or "change" in demand indicates the *curve itself has shifted*

    2.) A "change in quantity demanded" indicates *movement along a static curve* (which outlines the current relationship between price and quantity demanded)

EXHIBIT 6: Shift in Demand vs. Change in Quantity Demanded

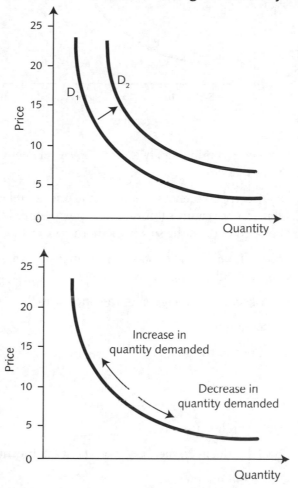

2. Supply

    a. Supply means the quantity of a good that businesses willingly produce and sell

    b. The supply curve for a commodity shows the relationship between its market price and the amount of that commodity producers are willing to produce and sell. The supply curve measures price on the vertical axis and quantities supplied on the horizontal axis.

EXHIBIT 7:   The Supply Curve

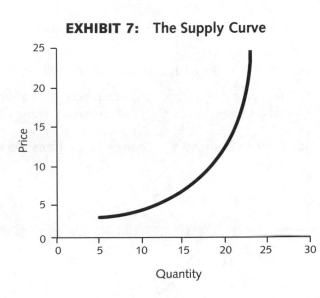

c. Main force determining supply is profit. A key element affecting supply decisions is the cost of production.

d. Another element influencing supply is the price of related goods. Related goods are goods that can be readily substituted for one another in the production process. If the price of one good rises, the supply of another substitute good is likely to decrease.

e. A reduction in tariffs and quotas on foreign goods will open the market to foreign producers and will tend to increase supply.

f. If a market becomes monopolized, the price at each level of output will increase.

g. Factors affecting supply

   1.) The price of the good

   2.) Technology

   3.) Input prices

   4.) Prices of related goods

   5.) Special influences, such as government tax incentives

3. Supply and demand interaction

   a. Market equilibrium comes at the price and quantity where the supply and demand forces are in balance (where the demand and supply curves intersect)

   b. Supply and demand can do more than illustrate the equilibrium price and quantity. They can be used to predict the impact of changes in economic conditions on prices and quantities.

   c. When factors underlying demand or supply change, shifts in demand or supply and changes in the market equilibrium of price and quantity occur

   d. Rationing by prices—by determining the equilibrium prices and quantities of all inputs and outputs, the market allocates (rations) the scarce goods of the society among the possible uses

4. Price elasticity of demand

   a. Price elasticity is the responsiveness of the quantity demanded of a good to changes in the good's price, other factors held constant

   b. The percentage change in quantity demanded is divided by the percentage change in price

   c. Elastic and inelastic demand—goods differ in their elasticities. Demand for necessities (e.g., food) responds little to price changes, whereas luxuries are generally highly price sensitive.

   d. A good is elastic when its quantity demanded responds greatly to price changes and inelastic when its quantity demanded responds little to price changes

   e. Unit-elastic demand occurs when the percentage change in quantity is exactly the same as the percentage change in price

   f. The slope is not the same as the elasticity because the demand curve's slope depends on the changes in price and quantity, whereas the elasticity depends on the percentage changes in price and quantity

   g. Elasticity and revenue—elasticity helps to clarify the impact of price changes on the total revenue of producers

   h. Total revenue

      1.) When demand is price inelastic, a price decrease reduces total revenue because quantity stays relatively constant

      2.) When demand is price elastic, a price decrease increases total revenue because quantity will increase significantly

      3.) In the case of unit-elastic demand, a price decrease leads to no change in total revenue

   i. Economic factors determine the magnitude of price elasticities for individual goods, the degree to which a good is a necessity or a luxury, the extent to which substitutes are available, the time available for response, and the relative importance of a commodity in the consumer's budget

   j. The price elasticity of supply measures the percentage change in quantity supplied in response to a 1% change in the good's price

B. INFLATION

1. Key terms:

   a. Inflation: an increase in the general level of prices

      1.) The inflation rate is the rate of change in the general price level

   b. Deflation: the opposite of inflation, this is a decline in general price levels and is often caused by a reduction in the money supply

   c. Disinflation: a decline in the inflation rate (e.g. a reduction in the rate at which prices rise)

2. Effects of inflation

   a. During periods of inflation, some, but not all, prices and wages move at the same rate

   b. A redistribution of income and wealth occurs among different classes. The major redistributive impact of inflation occurs through its effect on the real value of people's wealth. In general, unanticipated inflation redistributes wealth from creditors to debtors (i.e., unanticipated or unforeseen inflation helps those who have borrowed money and hurts those who have lent money). An unanticipated decline in inflation has the opposite effect.

   c. Changes are created in the relative prices and outputs of different goods or sometimes in output and employment for the economy as a whole

3. Real interest rate adjustment—inflation persists for a long time, and markets begin to adapt. An allowance for inflation is generally built into the market interest rate.

4. Inflation affects the real economy in two specific areas: total output and economic efficiency

5. There is no necessary relationship between prices and output

6. Inflation may be associated with either a higher or a lower level of output and employment

7. Generally, the higher the inflation rate, the greater the changes in relative prices

8. Distortions occur when prices get out of line relative to costs and demands

9. Measures of inflation

   a. A price index is a weighted average of the prices of numerous goods and services. The most well known price indexes are the Consumer Price Index (CPI), the gross domestic product (GDP) deflator, and the Producer Price Index (PPI).

      1.) The Consumer Price Index (CPI) measures the market cost of a basket of consumer goods and services, including prices of food, clothing, shelter, fuels, transportation, medical care, college tuition, and other commodities purchased for day-to-day living

         a.) A price index is constructed by weighting each price according to the economic importance of the commodity in question

         b.) Each item is assigned a fixed weight proportional to its relative importance in consumer expenditure budgets

      2.) The GDP deflator is a broader price index than the CPI

         a.) Measures the change in the average price of the market basket of goods included in GDP

            ■ Gross domestic product (GDP)—the total market value of all goods and services produced within the domestic United States over the course of a given year, including income generated domestically by a foreign firm

         b.) In addition to consumer goods, the GDP deflator includes prices for capital goods and other goods and services purchased by businesses and governments

         c.) This measure also separates increases in productivity from inflation increases

3.) The Producer Price Index (PPI) measures the average change over time in selling prices received by domestic producers of goods and services

   a.) PPIs measure price change from the perspective of the seller (opposite of the CPI)

4.) Index-number problems

   a.) Cost of living may be overestimated because consumers substitute relatively inexpensive goods for relatively expensive ones

   b.) CPI does not accurately capture changes in quality of goods

   c.) Although the CPI is modified from time to time, it is not corrected for quality improvements

C. MONETARY AND FISCAL POLICY

1. Monetary policy

   a. The Federal Reserve Bank (Fed) controls the money supply, enabling it to significantly affect interest rates. The Fed will follow a loose, or easy, monetary policy when it wants to increase the money supply to expand the level of income and employment. In times of inflation and when it wants to constrict the money supply, the Fed will follow a tight monetary policy.

   1.) Expansionary (easy) monetary policy—the supply of money increases, resulting in the circulation of more money. This leads to more funds available for banks to lend and ultimately to a decline in interest rates.

   2.) Restrictive (tight) monetary policy—the supply of money is restricted, resulting in less money available for banks to lend. This leads to an increase in interest rates.

   b. The Fed has several methods of controlling the money supply

   1.) Reserve requirements—the reserve requirement for a member bank of the Federal Reserve Bank is the percentage of deposit liabilities that must be held in reserve. As this requirement is increased, less money is available to be loaned to customers, resulting in a restriction of the money supply.

   2.) Federal Reserve discount rate

   a.) This is the rate at which member banks can borrow funds from the Federal Reserve to meet reserve requirements

   b.) When the Fed raises the discount rate, it increases the borrowing cost and discourages member banks from borrowing funds, resulting in a contraction of the money supply

   c.) The Fed will lower the discount rate when it wants to increase the money supply. Banks are able to borrow funds at lower rates and lend more money, which increases the supply.

   NOTE: The discount rate is the borrowing rate from the Federal Reserve, and the Fed Funds Rate is the overnight lending rate between member banks.

3.)   Open market operations

   a.)   Method most commonly used to control the money supply

   b.)   This is the process that the Federal Reserve follows to purchase and sell government securities in the open market

   c.)   The Fed will buy government securities to cause more money to circulate, thus increasing lending and lowering interest rates

   d.)   The Fed will sell government securities to restrict the money supply. As investors purchase government securities, more money leaves circulation, which decreases lending and increases interest rates.

   e.)   The Federal Open Market Committee (FOMC) is in charge of open market operations. The FOMC is made up of a rotation membership of Federal Reserve banks with the Federal Reserve Bank of New York, which is a permanent member.

   ■   An easy way to remember Open Market Operations is the BEST acronym: "**B**uy-**E**asy-**S**ell-**T**ight"

ANALYZE AND APPLY

Your client, Carlos, would like to refinance his home. There is no reason for him to do so immediately, so he has come to you for advice. You have recently read that in the near future the Federal Reserve Board (Fed) is planning on expanding economic activity using government securities. Regarding the timing of his refinancing, what would you recommend Carlos do?

A.   Wait for the money supply to decrease and interest rates to fall as is expected when the Fed buys government securities to expand economic activity

B.   Wait for the money supply to increase and interest rates to fall as is expected when the Fed buys government securities to expand economic activity

C.   Wait for the money supply to increase and interest rates to fall as is expected when the Fed sells government securities to expand economic activity

D.   Refinance now because the money supply will decrease and interest rates will increase when the Fed sells government securities to expand economic activity

Answer: B. If the Fed wants to expand economic activity using government securities, it will put more money into the economy by purchasing government securities. This will decrease interest rates, thus stimulating the economy. Therefore, Carlos should wait for rates to fall before refinancing his home. Even though the money supply will decrease and interest rates will increase when the Fed sells government securities, this will decrease economic activity, which is not what the Fed is planning to do. (Domain 3 – Analyzing and Evaluating the Client's Current Financial Status)

2. Fiscal policy

   a. Collectively, taxation, expenditures, and debt management of the federal government are called fiscal policy. Economic growth, price stability, and full employment are goals that may be pursued by changes in fiscal policy. Fiscal policy is primarily controlled by Congress.

      1.) Expansionary (easy) fiscal policy—when the government increases purchases of goods and services while holding its revenues constant, it creates a budget deficit and stimulates aggregate demand

      2.) Restrictive (tight) fiscal policy—when the government either reduces its expenditures of goods and services or raises taxes, it causes a budget surplus or a reduction in the budget deficit

   b. Changes in taxation will affect corporate earnings, disposable earnings, and the overall economy

      1.) As tax rates increase, corporations' after-tax income declines, which reduces their ability to pay dividends. This may cause the price for equities to decrease.

      2.) Tax increases also reduce individuals' disposable income and limit the amount of money entering the economy

      3.) The demand for tax-free investments is also influenced by changes in taxation. As increases in taxes occur, the attractiveness of tax-free instruments also increases.

   c. Government expenditures—corporate earnings benefit from increases in government expenditures

   d. Deficit spending—deficit spending occurs when expenditures exceed revenues of the government. By selling securities to the public to finance deficits, the Treasury competes with other securities. This drives prices down. The decrease in price causes yields to rise.

3. The nature of interest rates

   a. The price of borrowing money is the interest rate

   b. The nominal interest rate measures the yield in dollars per year per dollar invested

   c. The *real* interest rate is the nominal rate adjusted for inflation. This is considered to be a more accurate measure of the true impact of the interest rate. Calculated as follows:

$$\left[\frac{1 + \text{nominal rate}}{1 + \text{inflation rate}} - 1 \right] \times 100 = \text{real rate of return}$$

   This is a key component in the calculation of education, retirement needs, and serial payments.

D. BUSINESS CYCLE THEORIES

1. Business cycles consist of swings in total national output, income, and employment marked by widespread expansion or contraction in many sectors of the economy

2. Business cycles generally occur as a result of shifts in aggregate demand. The cycle consists of two phases—expansion and contraction—and two points—peak and trough.

   a. The expansion phase comes to an end and goes into the contraction phase at the upper turning point, or peak

   b. Similarly, the contraction phase gives way to expansion at the lower turning point, or trough. The emphasis here is not so much on high or low business activity as on the dynamic aspects of rising or falling business activity.

3. Business cycles are affected by the growth or decline in the gross domestic product (GDP), which is the total market value of all goods and services within the domestic United States over the course of a given year, including income generated domestically by a foreign firm

4. Definitions

   a. Peak—the point at the end of the expansion phase when most businesses are operating at capacity and gross domestic product (GDP) is increasing rapidly. The peak is the point at which GDP is at its highest point and exceeds the long-run average GDP. Usually, employment peaks at this point.

   b. Trough—the point at the end of the contraction phase where businesses are operating at their lowest capacity levels. Unemployment is rapidly increasing and peaks because sales fall rapidly. GDP growth is at its lowest or negative.

   c. Contraction phase—leads to trough. Business sales fall. Unemployment increases. GDP growth falls.

   d. Expansion phase—leads to peak. Business sales rise. GDP grows. Unemployment declines. Also called recovery phase.

   e. Recession—a decline in real GDP for two or more successive quarters characterized by the following:

      1.) Consumer purchases decline

      2.) Business inventories expand

      3.) GDP falls

      4.) Capital investment falls

      5.) Demand for labor falls

      6.) Unemployment is high

      7.) Commodity prices fall

      8.) Business profits fall

      9.) Interest rates fall as a result of reduced demand for money

   f. Depression—persistent recession and a severe decline in economic activity

EXHIBIT 8: General Business Cycles

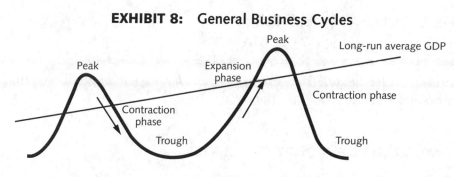

NOTE: The business cycle is not symmetrical as drawn. The pattern of the business cycle is irregular and unpredictable.

5. The business cycle is a dynamic system with each cycle passing into the next.

   a. Each is characterized by different conditions that may be reflective of the current or upcoming cycle.

6. Capital formation—certain economic variables always show greater fluctuations than others in the business cycle

7. Durable goods (goods not for immediate consumption and have usefulness for a period of time)—subject to violently erratic patterns of demand. The durable or capital goods sector of the economy shows, by far, the greatest cyclical fluctuations.

8. Leading indicators—used to predict changes in the business cycle because they tend to precede and anticipate any changes. Bond yields, housing starts, investor sentiment, and durable goods orders are examples of leading indicators.

9. Coincident indicators—occur simultaneously during the business cycle in order to confirm the current state of the economy or cycle. Examples include level of unemployment, consumer income, industrial production, and profits.

10. Lagging indicators—change after the economy has shifted to another stage of the business cycle. Examples include the average duration of unemployment and the prime interest rate.

11. GDP versus GNP

   a. Gross domestic product (GDP)—GDP (or nominal GDP) is the total monetary value of goods and services produced within a country's border over the course of a year. Measures the health of a country's economy and standard of living. Real GDP is an inflation adjusted GDP figure in constant dollars.

   b. Gross national product (GNP)—GNP includes income generated by domestic individuals both domestically and internationally; however, unlike GDP, it does not include income generated domestically by a foreign firm. Measured in constant dollars.

VIII.   TIME VALUE OF MONEY

CFP Board Principal Knowledge Topic B.13.

Refer to the *Understanding Your Financial Calculator* book for additional time value of money examples and practice questions

A.   TIME VALUE OF MONEY CONCEPTS

1. Concepts

   a. A dollar received today is worth more than a dollar received one year from today because the dollar received today can be invested and will be worth more in one year

   b. Alternatively, a dollar to be received a year from now is currently worth less than a dollar today

2. Future value

   a. Future dollar amount to which a sum certain today will increase compounded at a defined interest rate and a period of time

3. Present value

   a. Current dollar value of a future sum discounted at a defined interest rate and a period of time

B.   FUTURE VALUE OF A SINGLE SUM

1. A dollar in hand today is worth more than a dollar to be received next year. If you had one dollar now, you could invest, earn interest, and have more than one dollar next year.

> **EXAMPLE**   Megan has an account valued at $100 today paying 10% interest compounded annually. At the end of year 1, Megan will have:
>
> PV = 100 = present value of her account, or the beginning amount.
> i = 10 = interest rate per period.
> FV_n = future value, or ending amount, of Megan's account at the end of n years.
> n = number of periods, often years, involved in the transaction.
> n = 1, so FV_n = FV_1, calculated as follows:
> The future value, FV, at the end of 1 period is the present value multiplied by 1 plus the interest rate. The equation can now be used to find how much Megan's $100 will be worth at the end of 1 year at a 10% interest rate:
> $FV_1 = 100 \times (1 + 0.10) = 100 \times (1.10) = 110$
> Megan's account will earn $10 of interest; therefore, she will have $110 at the end of the year.

2. Solving future value problems

    a. Financial calculators can solve most cash flow problems. The calculators generate the future value interest factors for a specified pair of i and n values, then multiply the computed factor by the PV to produce the FV.

    b. For example, enter PV = 100, i = 10, and n = 5, and press the FV key. The answer, −161.0510, rounded to four decimal places, is displayed. (Always round to four decimal places.) The FV will appear with a minus sign on most calculators. This is simply calculator logic.

    c. Some calculators may require you to press the Compute key before pressing the FV button. Financial calculators permit you to specify the number of decimal places. Use at least two places for problems where the answer is in dollars or percentages and four when you are solving for the interest rate.

EXAMPLE Erin invested $10,000 in an interest-bearing account earning an 11% annual rate compounded monthly. At the end of 7 years, the account will be worth $21,522.04, assuming all interest is reinvested at the 11% rate.

PV = 10,000
i = 0.9167 (11 ÷ 12)
n = 84 (7 × 12)
Solve for FV = 21,522.0361, or $21,522.04

Keystrokes for the HP 10bII/HP 10bII+:

Keystrokes	Display
10000[i/]	10,000
[PV]	−10,000.0000
11÷12=[I/YR]	0.9167
7x12=[N]	84.0000
[FV]	**21,522.0361**

The PV is entered as a negative number to represent Erin's investment. The logic behind the negative value is that the initial amount (PV) is an *outflow* to Erin, and the future value (FV) is an *inflow* (positive value) to Erin.

C. PRESENT VALUE OF A SINGLE SUM

1. This calculation is used to determine what a sum of money to be received in a future year is worth in today's dollars on the basis of a specific discount rate

2. A financial calculator could be used to find the PV of the $161.05 calculated in the previous future value example. Just enter n = 5, i = 10, and FV = 161.05, and press the PV button to find PV = 100. On some calculators, the PV will be given as −100, and on some calculators, you must press the Compute key before pressing the PV key.

E X A M P L E   Nick's coin collection is currently worth $100,000. He purchased the coins five years ago, and they have appreciated 8% per year. Calculate how much he paid five years ago by solving for the present value (PV).

FV = 100,000
$i = 8$
$n = 5$
Solve for PV = –68,058.3197, or $68,058.32

Keystrokes for the HP 10bII/HP 10bII+:

Keystrokes	Display
100000	100,000
[FV]	100,000.0000
8[I/YR]	8.0000
5[N]	5.0000
[PV]	–68,058.3197

Here, the current value of the coin collection is entered as a FV, as it is a FV in relation to Nick's original investment (PV). The FV is entered as a positive value to Nick, and the amount he originally paid for the coin collection is a negative value, as it is an outflow (investment) by Nick.

D. SOLVING FOR TIME AND INTEREST RATES

1. Solving for period (n)

    a. Applications

        1.) Answers the question of how long (in months, quarters, or years) to save or pay to accomplish some goal, if the amount is saved or paid at a given rate

        2.) Useful in debt management, such as determining the term to:

            a.) Pay off student loans

            b.) Pay off mortgage

            c.) Save for college education

            d.) Save for a special purchase (e.g., car, home, vacation)

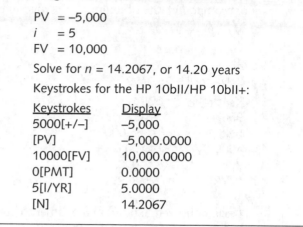

EXAMPLE How long will it take $5,000 to grow to $10,000, assuming a 5% annual interest rate?

PV = –5,000

i = 5

FV = 10,000

Solve for n = 14.2067, or 14.20 years

Keystrokes for the HP 10bII/HP 10bII+:

Keystrokes	Display
5000[+/–]	–5,000
[PV]	–5,000.0000
10000[FV]	10,000.0000
0[PMT]	0.0000
5[I/YR]	5.0000
[N]	14.2067

NOTE: The HP12c calculator rounds N to a whole number. If you need a more precise number, you will need to reach it through trial and error. Refer to the *Understanding Your Financial Calculator* book for details.

Once you have finished the calculation using a financial calculator, re-enter the n and calculate the FV to assure yourself that the n calculated is correct to the precise degree that you require (e.g., two decimal places).

2. Solving for interest rate (i)

    a. Determines the interest rate paid or received on an investment

E X A M P L E S   Joe purchased 100 shares of an aggressive growth mutual fund at $9 per share 7 years ago. Today, he sold all 100 shares for $4,500. His average annual compound rate of return on this investment before tax was 25.85%.

PV = (900)
FV = 4,500
n = 7
Solve for i = 25.8499

Keystrokes	Display
900[+/−]	−900
[PV]	−900.0000
4500[FV]	4,500.0000
7[N]	7.0000
[I/YR]	25.8499

Leslie borrowed $800 from her father to purchase a mountain bike. Leslie paid back $1,200 to her father at the end of 5 years. The average annual compound rate of interest on Leslie's loan from her father was 8.45%.

PV = 800
FV = (1,200)
n = 5
Solve for i = 8.4472

Keystrokes	Display
800	800
[PV]	800.0000
1200[+/−][FV]	−1,200.0000
5[N]	5.0000
[I/YR]	8.4472

E.   FUTURE VALUE OF AN ANNUITY

1. An annuity is a series of equal payments at fixed intervals for a specified number of periods. Payments are given the symbol PMT.

2. If the payments occur at the end of each period, they are referred to as an *ordinary annuity*

3. If the payments are made at the beginning of each period, they are referred to as an *annuity due* (e.g., lease or rent payment)

EXAMPLE—ORDINARY ANNUITY A promise to pay $1,000 a year for 3 years is a 3-year annuity. If each payment is made at the end of the year, it is an ordinary annuity. Patty receives such an annuity and deposits each annual payment into an account that pays 10% interest. How much will Patty have at the end of 3 years?

PMT_{OA} = 1,000
n = 3
i = 10
PV = 0

Solve for FV_{OA} = 3,310, or $3,310

Keystrokes for the HP 10bII/HP 10bII+:

Keystrokes	Display
1000[+/−]	−1,000
[PMT]	−1,000.0000
3[N]	3.0000
10[I/YR]	10.0000
0[PV]	0.0000
[FV]	3,310.0000

EXAMPLE—ANNUITY DUE Had Patty's three $1,000 payments in the previous example been made at the beginning of each year, the annuity would have been an annuity due.

PMT_{AD} = 1,000
n = 3
i = 10
PV   = 0

Solve for FV_{AD} = 3,641, or $3,641

Keystrokes for the HP 10bII/HP 10bII+:

Keystrokes	Display
[■] [BEG/END]	
1000[+/−]	−1,000
[PMT]	−1,000.0000
3[N]	3.0000
10[I/YR]	10.0000
0[PV]	0.0000
[FV]	3,641.0000

E X A M P L E — A N N U I T Y   D U E   Christine has been dollar cost averaging into a mutual fund by investing $2,000 at the beginning of every quarter for the past 7 years. She has been earning an average annual return of 11% compounded quarterly on this investment. Today, the fund is worth $84,996.80.

$$PMT_{AD} = 2,000$$
$$i = 2.75\ (11 \div 4)$$
$$n = 28\ (7 \times 4)$$
Solve for FV_{AD} = 84,996.8045, or $84,996.80

Keystrokes	Display
[■] [BEG/END]	
2000[+/−]	−2,000
[PMT]	−2,000.0000
7×4=[N]	28.0000
11÷4=[I/YR]	2.7500
0[PV]	0.0000
[FV]	84,996.8045

Note: This is an FV problem because the future value of Christine's quarterly investments is the value of the fund today.

F.   PRESENT VALUE OF AN ANNUITY

1. The difference between the present value of an annuity due and the present value of an ordinary annuity is that the annuity due's payments are made at the beginning of each period rather than at the end, as for an ordinary annuity

2. This makes the present value of an annuity due always larger than the present value of an ordinary annuity with the same payments

3. This calculation is most often used for education funding and for retirement capital needs analysis

E X A M P L E — O R D I N A R Y   A N N U I T Y   Sherri is offered the following alternatives: (1) a 3-year annuity with payments of $1,000 at the end of each year or (2) a lump-sum payment today. She has no need for the money during the next 3 years, and if she accepts the annuity, she would deposit the payments in an account that pays 10% interest. Similarly, the lump-sum payment would be deposited in an account paying 10%. How large must the lump-sum payment be to make it equivalent to the annuity?

$$PMT_{OA} = 1,000$$
$$n = 3$$
$$i = 10$$
Solve for PV_{OA} = 2,486.8520, or $2,486.85

Keystrokes	Display
1000[+/−]	−1,000
[PMT]	−1,000.0000
3[N]	3.0000
10[I/YR]	10.0000
0[FV]	0.0000
[PV]	2,486.8520

Therefore, the lump-sum payment must be equal to or greater than $2,486.85 if the $1,000 is paid at the end of each year.

EXAMPLE—ANNUITY DUE Abby wants to withdraw $4,000 at the beginning of each year for the next 7 years. She expects to earn 10.5% compounded annually on her investment. The lump sum Abby should deposit today is $21,168.72.

PMT_{AD} =   4,000
i =   10.5
n =   7

Solve for PV_{AD} = 21,168.7176, or $21,168.72

Keystrokes	Display
[■] [BEG/END]	
4000[+/−]	−4,000
[PMT]	−4,000.0000
10.5[I/YR]	10.5000
7[N]	7.0000
0[FV]	0.0000
[PV]	21,168.7176

Note: If you calculated $19,157.21 as PV, your calculator is on END mode. Set to BEG mode to calculate the correct PV.

G. CALCULATING PAYMENT (PMT)

1. When solving for PMT, the present value (PV), future value (FV), interest rate (i), and number of payments (n) must be known.

2. Pay attention to the timing of the payment (beginning of period – annuity due, end of period – ordinary annuity).

EXAMPLE If Linda invests $15,000 and earns 7% on her investment, compounded quarterly, what is the amount of payment she would receive at the beginning of each quarter over six years?

PV = (15,000)
n = 24 (6 x 4)
i = 1.75 (7 ÷ 4)
FV = 0

Solve for PMT_{AD} = 757.5280, or $757.53

Keystrokes	Display
[■] [BEG/END]	
15000[+/−]	−15,000
[PV]	−15,000.0000
6×4=[N]	24.0000
7÷4=[I/YR]	1.7500
[FV]	0.0000
[PMT]	757.5280

ANALYZE AND APPLY

1. Carter and Claire Brown met with Evan, a CFP® professional, requesting that he analyze the effect a new home purchase would have on their cash flow. They are planning on purchasing a home for $400,000 with a 30% down payment. They will finance the purchase with a fixed 30-year mortgage with a 4% interest rate. What would be the most appropriate steps Evan should take and in what order?

   1. Obtain information regarding the new home and property taxes for the area in which it is located
   2. Advise the Browns that if the interest rate is lower than the interest on their current mortgage, they can assume their cash flow will be improved
   3. Calculate the Brown's new mortgage payment (PITI) and prepare an updated statement of cash flows for the couple
   4. Advise the Browns that the principal and interest payment would not be the only outflow affected by the purchase of the new home

   A. 2 only
   B. 1, 3
   C. 2, 3, 1
   D. 4, 1, 3

   Answer: D. Evan should make the Browns aware that several expenses could change as a result of purchasing a new home (e.g., taxes, insurance, and utilities). Evan should obtain information regarding the Brown's new monthly tax and insurance payments, so he can get an accurate estimate of the new mortgage payment. With this amount, he can prepare an updated statement of cash flows for the couple. He should also advise the Browns that their statement of cash flows should be updated once they move into their new home and are more certain of their new outflows. Statement 2 is incorrect because it cannot always be assumed that a lower interest rate will translate into a lower mortgage payment and, therefore, an improved cash flow. Several variables will influence the payment amount (e.g., the term or amount of the new mortgage). (Domain 3 – Analyzing and Evaluating the Client's Current Status)

2. Gavin and Anna, your clients, are purchasing one of two new homes, each valued at $200,000. The financing available for each home is as follows:

Mortgage – Home #1		Mortgage – Home #2	
Down payment	30%	Down payment	10%
Term	15 yrs	Term	30 yrs
Fixed interest rate	5%	Fixed interest rate	6.5%

The couple has come to you, their financial planner, requesting that you analyze these two mortgage options. They would like to purchase the home with the financing that will result in the lowest monthly principal and interest payment. What should you advise Gavin and Anna?

A. The monthly payment for Home #1 is approximately $31 lower than the monthly payment for Home #2.

B. The monthly payment for Home #2 is approximately $128 lower than the monthly payment for Home #1.

C. The monthly payment for Home #1 is approximately $318 higher than the monthly payment for Home #2.

D. The monthly payment for Home #2 is approximately $444 higher than the monthly payment for Home #1.

Answer: A. One might think that the monthly mortgage payment for Home #1 would be higher because its term is half the term on Home #2. However, because the mortgage principal and interest rate for the Home #1 mortgage is so much lower, the mortgage payment for Home #1 is actually $31 less than Home 2.

Mortgage Payment - Home #1		Mortgage Payment - Home #2	
Mortgage principal (PV)	140,000	Mortgage principal (PV)	180,000
Term in months (n)	180 (15 x 12)	Term in months (n)	360 (30 x 12)
Monthly interest rate (i)	0.4167 (5 ÷ 12)	Monthly interest rate (i)	0.5417 (6.5 ÷ 12)
Balance at end of term (FV)	0	Balance at end of term (FV)	0
Solve for PMT	1,107.11	Solve for PMT	1,137.72

$1,137.72 (House #2 PMT) – $1,107.11 (House #1 PMT) = $30.61, rounded to $31. (Domain 3 – Analyzing and Evaluating the Client's Current Status)

H. SERIAL PAYMENTS

1. A serial payment is a payment that increases at some constant rate (usually inflation) on a regular basis. There are many situations where it is more affordable to increase payments on an annual basis because the payor expects to have increases in cash flows or earnings to make those increasing payments (e.g., life insurance, education needs, or retirement needs).

2. Serial payments differ from fixed annuity payments (both ordinary and annuity due payments) in that serial payments are not a fixed amount per year. Thus, the initial serial payment is less than its respective annuity due or ordinary annuity payment. The last serial payment will obviously be greater than the last respective fixed annuity payment but will have the same purchasing power as the first serial payment.

3. The serial payment is calculated by using an inflation-adjusted interest rate formula:

$$\{[(1 + r) \div (1 + i)] - 1\} \times 100$$

r = rate of return of an investment

i = assumed annual inflation rate

a. Accordingly, this becomes the interest rate (I/YR) that is entered into your HP 10bII/HP 10bII+ calculator

b. Then, when you know the required value in today's dollars and the number of years to achieve this value, you can determine the resulting payment

c. The second year's payment is then increased by the assumed rate of inflation, and so on

---

EXAMPLE—CALCULATION OF A SERIAL PAYMENT

Clark needs to save $50,000 (in today's dollars) for his son's college expenses in 5 years. He wants to assume an inflation rate of 4% and an investment rate of return of 8%. If the required payments are made at the end of each year, he needs to save $9,630.17 in the first year, calculated as follows:

- 50,000 FV
- 5 N
- 3.8462 I/YR [(1.08 ÷ 1.04) – 1] × 100 = 3.8462 (inflation-adjusted)
- Solve for PMT = 9,259.7823, or $9,259.78

Because the payments are made at the end of each year, the calculated payment of $9,259.78 must be inflated by 4%. Therefore, to derive the end of the first year payment, multiply $9,259.78 by 1.04. This results in an end of year payment of $9,630.17.

All 5 payments are as follows:
$9,259.78 × 1.04 = $9,630.17
$9,630.17 × 1.04 = $10,015.38
$10,015.38 × 1.04 = $10,415.99
$10,415.99 × 1.04 = $10,832.63
$10,832.63 × 1.04 = $11,265.94

I.   NET PRESENT VALUE

1. Net present value (NPV) analysis is a common technique used by businesses and investors to evaluate capital projects and capital expenditures, generally in the capital budgeting area

2. To calculate NPV:

a. Start with the amount and timing of future cash flows (including the eventual sale of the investment)

b. These future cash flows are then discounted by the required rate of return—resulting in a present value of the future cash flows

c. The purchase price is netted against this, and the result is the NPV of the asset

> **E X A M P L E**   If the present value of a series of cash inflows is $200 and the initial outflow is $150, the NPV equals $50 ($200 – $150). An NPV greater than zero implies that the IRR of the cash flows is greater than the discount rate used to discount the future cash flows. An NPV of zero implies that the discount rate used is equal to the IRR for the cash flows. A negative NPV implies that the discount rate used is greater than the true IRR of the cash flows. As a general rule, you should look for investments that have a positive NPV.

3. Internal rate of return (IRR)—discount rate that makes the present value (PV) of the cash inflows equal to the initial cash outflows such that the net present value (NPV) is equal to zero

> **E X A M P L E**   Benjamin, an industrious teenager, is starting a small business that requires an initial cash investment of $5,000. He expects the following cash flows:
>
> | End of year | Cash flow |
> |:---:|:---:|
> | 1 | $500 |
> | 2 | $800 |
> | 3 | $1,000 |
> | 4 | $1,000 |
> | 5 | $200 |
>
> If he sells his business at the end of year 5 for $3,000, what is his internal rate of return (IRR) for his business investment?
>
> | Keystrokes | Display |
> |---|---|
> | 5000[+/–] | –5,000 |
> | [CFj] | –5,000.0000 |
> | 500[CFj] | 500.0000 |
> | 800[CFj] | 800.0000 |
> | 1000[CFj] | 1,000.0000 |
> | 2[■][Nj] | 2.0000 |
> | 200[+] | 200.0000 |
> | 3000[=] | 3,200.0000 (3,200 = year 5 cash flow of 200 plus the ending value of 3,000) |
> | [CFj] | 3,200.0000 |
> | [■][IRR/YR] | 7.1533 |

4. NPV is considered a superior model to IRR when comparing investment projects of unequal lives

   a. NPV helps a company decide whether to buy a particular piece of equipment or make a particular investment

5. The result of NPV calculation is expressed in dollars (rather than a percent)

6. NPV equals the difference between the initial cash outflow (investment) and the present value of discounted cash inflows

---

If NPV > 0, IRR > required rate of return

If NPV = 0, IRR = required rate of return

If NPV < 0, IRR < required rate of return

IX.   FINANCIAL SERVICES REGULATIONS AND REQUIREMENTS

CFP Board Principal Knowledge Topic A.4.

A.   INTRODUCTION

1. The issuance and sale of corporate securities are extensively regulated by the Securities and Exchange Commission (SEC), a federal agency that administers the Securities Act of 1933, the Securities Exchange Act of 1934, and other federal statutes

2. A major objective of securities regulation is to protect the investing public by requiring full and fair disclosure of relevant information

3. Both federal and state governments require a substantial amount of regulation; however, most regulation is from the federal government because the majority of trading is done across state borders

B.   FEDERAL SECURITIES REGULATION

1. Securities Act of 1933

   a. Primarily concerned with *new issues* of securities ("primary market")

   b. Two objectives:

      1.) Require investors receive financial and other significant information concerning securities being offered for public sale

      2.) Prohibit deceit, misrepresentations, and other fraud in the sale of securities

   c. Requires that securities sold in the United States must be registered with the SEC.

   d. A registration statement contains a thorough description of the securities; the financial structure, condition, and management personnel of the issuing corporation; and a description of material pending litigation against the issuing corporation

   e. Requires that a prospectus based on the information in the registration statement be given to any prospective investor or purchaser

   f. Registration statements and prospectuses become public shortly after filing with the SEC

   g. Securities that are exempt from registration requirements

      1.) Intrastate offerings

      2.) Securities of municipal, state, and federal governments

      3.) Offerings of limited size

         a.) Promotes capital formation by lowering the cost of offering securities to the public

      4.) Private offerings to a limited number of persons or institutions

2. Glass-Steagall Act (1933)

   a.   Prohibited commercial banks from acting as investment bankers

   b.   Established the Federal Deposit Insurance Corporation (FDIC)

   c.   Prohibited commercial banks from paying interest on demand deposits

3. Securities Exchange Act of 1934

   a.   Whereas the 1933 Act was limited to new issues, the 1934 Act extended the regulation to securities *sold in the secondary market*; the Act provided the following provisions

      1.)   Establishment of the SEC—the SEC's primary function is to regulate the securities markets

      2.)   Disclosure requirements for secondary market—annual reports and other financial reports are required to be filed with the SEC prior to listing on the organized exchanges.

      3.)   Registration of *organized exchanges*

      4.)   Proxy solicitation—specific rules governing solicitation of proxies were established

      5.)   Exemptions—securities of federal, state, and local governments; securities that are not traded across state lines; and any other securities specified by the SEC are exempt from registering with the SEC.

      6.)   Insider trading—illegal when a person trades a security while in possession of material nonpublic information in violation of a duty to withhold the information or refrain from trading.

         a.)   A public report, called an insider report, must be filed with the SEC for every month in which a change in the holding of a firm's securities occurs for an officer, director, or 10% or more shareholder.

         b.)   The 1934 Act forbids insiders profiting from securities held less than six months and requires these profits be returned to the organization.

         c.)   Short sales are not permitted by individuals considered to be insiders.

4. Investment Company Act of 1940 requires registration with the SEC and restricts activities of investment companies (including mutual funds)

5. Maloney Act of 1938—brought the OTC market under the regulation of the SEC and called for self-regulation of OTC securities dealers

6. Federal Bankruptcy Act of 1938

   a.   As amended in 1978, requires a court-appointed trustee to oversee the affairs of a firm for which bankruptcy charges have been filed

   b.   Provides for the liquidation of hopelessly troubled firms and provides for the reorganization of troubled firms that may be able to survive

7. Investment Advisers Act of 1940

   a.   Regulates investment advisers

b. Requires that firms or sole practitioners compensated for advising others about securities must register with the SEC and follow regulations aimed at protecting investors

c. Generally, only advisers who have at least $100 million of assets under management or advise a registered investment company must register with the SEC

8. McCarran Ferguson Act of 1945—clarified that insurance was to be regulated at the state level

9. Securities Investor Protection Act of 1970—established the Securities Investor Protection Corporation (SIPC) to insure investors against losses arising from the failure of any brokerage firm

10. Financial Services Modernization Act of 1999 (Gramm-Leach-Bliley Act)

a. Repeals sections of the Glass-Steagall Act that prohibited a bank holding company and a securities firm that underwrites and deals in ineligible securities from owning and controlling each other

b. Also amends the Bank Holding Company Act of 1956 to permit cross-ownership and control among bank holding companies, securities firms, and insurance companies, provided that such cross-ownership and control is effected through a financial holding company that engages in activities that conform to the act

11. Sarbanes-Oxley Act of 2002

a. Includes reforms for corporate responsibility, increased financial disclosure requirements, and reduced corporate and accounting fraud

b. Created the Public Company Accounting Oversight Board to oversee the auditing profession

12. Dodd-Frank Wall Street Reform and Consumer Protection Act of 2010

a. Reformed the U.S. regulatory system in a number of areas including consumer protection, trading restrictions, credit ratings, regulation of financial products, corporate governance, disclosure, and transparency

b. Modified the Investment Advisers Act of 1940 thresholds for registration with the SEC

1.) *Small advisers*—those with less than $25 million of assets under management (AUM) are regulated by one or more states unless the state in which the adviser has its principal office and place of business has not enacted a statute regulating advisers

2.) *Mid-sized advisers*—those with between $25 million and $100 million of AUM are regulated by one of more state if (i) the adviser is registered with the state where it has its principal office and place of business, and (ii) the adviser is "subject to examination" by that state authority

3.) *Large advisers*—those with more than $100 million of AUM must register with the SEC (unless an exemption is available), and state adviser laws are pre-empted for these advisers. (Note that special transitional rules apply to advisers whose AUM fluctuates between $90–$110 million.)

13. State regulation of securities (blue-sky laws)—state securities laws also regulate the offering and sale of securities in intrastate commerce

    a. Antifraud provisions similar to federal laws

    b. Regulation of brokers and dealers in securities

    c. Registration and disclosure are required before securities can be offered for sale

    d. Some state statutes impose standards of fairness

    e. Some state statutes are more restrictive than the federal statutes and SEC rules

C. FINRA (FINANCIAL INDUSTRY REGULATORY AUTHORITY)

1. Persons wanting to sell securities must be registered with FINRA

2. Self-regulated organization

    a. Responsibility delegated to FINRA by the SEC

EXHIBIT 9:   Common FINRA Licenses for Registered Representatives

Securities Transaction/Activity	Qualification	Registration Requirement
Mutual funds (known as open-end funds); initial offering of closed-end funds; variable annuities; variable life insurance; unit investment trusts (initial offering only)	Investment Company Products/Variable Contracts Limited Representative	Series 6
Corporate securities (stocks and bonds); rights; warrants; mutual funds; money market funds; unit investment trusts; REITs; asset-backed securities; mortgage-backed securities; options; options on mortgage-backed securities; municipal securities; government securities; repos and certificates of accrual on government securities; direct participation programs; securities traders; mergers and acquisitions; venture capital; corporate financing	General Securities Representative	Series 7
Both the Series 65 and Series 66 exams were developed by the North American Securities Administrators Association (NASAA) and administered by FINRA Regulation. Unlike FINRA exams, such as the Series 6 and 7, an individual need not be sponsored by a broker/dealer.	Investment Adviser Representative	Series 65/66

D. REGULATION

1. The Securities and Exchange Commission (SEC) regulates investment advisers and their activities under the Investment Advisers Act of 1940

    a. Unless exempt under specific provisions of the act, a person covered by the act must register with the SEC as an investment adviser

2. The SEC is responsible for monitoring Registered Investment Advisors

3. Definition—an investment adviser is a person who does any of the following:

    a. Provides advice or issues reports or analyses regarding securities

    b. Is in the business of providing such services

    c. Provides such services for compensation

        1.) Compensation is the receipt of any economic benefit that includes commissions on the sale of products

2.)   Certain organizations and individuals are excluded

    a.)   Banks and bank holding companies (except as amended by the Gramm-Leach-Bliley Act of 1999)

    b.)   Lawyers, accountants, engineers, or teachers, if their performance of advisory services is solely incidental to their professions

    c.)   Brokers or dealers, if their performance of advisory services is solely incidental to the conduct of their business as brokers or dealers and they do not receive any special compensation for their advisory services

    d.)   Publishers of bona fide newspapers, newsmagazines, or business or financial publications of general and regular circulation

    e.)   Persons whose advice is related only to securities that are direct obligations of or guaranteed by the United States

    f.)   Incidental practice exception is not available to individuals who hold themselves out to the public as providing financial planning, pension consulting, or other financial advisory services

4. Exemptions

  a.   An intrastate adviser for unlisted securities

  b.   An adviser whose only clients are insurance companies

  c.   Foreign private advisers

  d.   Charitable organizations and plans

  e.   Commodity trading advisors

  f.   Private fund advisers

  g.   Venture capital advisers

  h.   Advisers to small business investment companies (SBICs)

5. Disclosure—the act generally requires investment advisers entering into an advisory contract with a client to deliver a written disclosure statement on their background and business practices.

  a.   The key document in making these disclosures is Part 2A of Form ADV, often referred to as the adviser's brochure (note that Form ADV Part 2A replaced Form ADV Part II in 2011)

    1.)   This document should clearly spell out the details of the advisory relationship and other business interests of the adviser

    2.)   This is the reference tool with which the client or potential client can compare advisory firms for cost of services and for compatibility with their needs

    3.)   Investment advisory regulations require that Part 2A of Form ADV or the brochure be given to customers in advance or no later than the time of entering into a contract if rescission is permitted within a specifically allotted time

b. An investment adviser shall deliver the statement required by this section to an advisory client or prospective advisory client (i) not less than 48 hours prior to entering into any written or oral investment advisory contract with such client or prospective client, or (ii) at the time of entering into any such contract, if the advisory client has a right to terminate the contract without penalty within five business days after entering into the contract

6. Inspections—the 1940 Adviser's Act and the SEC's rules require that advisers maintain and preserve specified books and records and make them available for inspection

7. Restriction on the use of the term *investment counsel*—a registered investment adviser may not use the term *investment counsel* unless its principal business is acting as an investment adviser and a substantial portion of its business is providing investment supervisory services

8. Antifraud provisions

   a. Prohibit misstatements or misleading omissions of material facts, fraudulent acts, and practices in connection with the purchase or sale of securities or the conduct of an investment advisory business

   b. An investment adviser owes his clients undivided loyalty and may not engage in activity that conflicts with a client's interest

9. Registration—Form ADV is kept current by filing periodic amendments; Form ADV-W is used to withdraw as an investment adviser

10. Filing requirements

   a. Forms—ADV and ADV-W

   b. Copies—all advisers' filings must be submitted in triplicate and typewritten. Copies can be filed, but each must be signed manually.

   c. Fees—must include a registration fee payable to the Securities and Exchange Commission, with initial application of Form ADV.

   d. Name and signatures—full names are required. Each copy of an execution page must contain an original manual signature.

E. PROFESSIONAL LIABILITY – FINANCIAL PLANNERS

1. Scope of responsibility

   a. As members of a profession, financial planners are expected to comply with standards of ethics and to perform their services in accordance with accepted principles and standards

   b. Financial planners who fail to perform these duties may be civilly liable to their clients, for whom they have agreed to provide services, and to third persons, who may have relied on statements prepared by them

   c. In addition, civil and criminal liability may be imposed on financial planners because of statutes, such as the federal securities laws

2. Potential common law liability to clients

   a. Liability based on *breach of contract*

      1.) If a financial planner has entered into a contract to perform certain services for a client and fails to honestly, properly, and completely perform those contractual duties, the financial planner will be civilly liable to the client for breach of contract

      2.) In most cases, if there has been a breach of contract by a financial planner, courts will award compensatory damages as a remedy to the client

   b. Liability based on *negligence*—a financial planner has a duty to exercise the same standard of care that a reasonably prudent and skillful financial planner in the community would exercise under the same or similar circumstances

   c. Liability based on *fraud*—in an action based on fraud, the client must establish that the financial planner

      1.) made a false representation of a material fact;

      2.) made the representation with knowledge that it was false (actual fraud) or with reckless disregard for its truth or falsity (constructive fraud);

      3.) intentionally made the misrepresentation to induce the client to act or not act; and

      4.) made the misrepresentation and the client was injured as a result of the client's reasonable reliance on the misrepresentation.

X.   CONSUMER PROTECTION LAWS

CFP Board Principal Knowledge Topic A.6.

A.   CREDIT PROTECTION

1. Federal Truth-in-Lending Act (Consumer Credit Protection Act) is administered by the Federal Reserve Board. Also known as Regulation Z.

    a. The act applies when:

    1.) A debtor is a natural person

    2.) The creditor in the ordinary course of its business is a lender, seller, or provider of services

    3.) The amount being financed is no more than $25,000 or is secured by real property, or by personal property used or expected to be used as the principal dwelling of the consumer

    b. Items that must be disclosed include annual percentage rate, finance charges, amount financed, number of payments, and any prepayment penalties

2. Fair Credit Billing Act

    a. A credit cardholder is given limited right to withhold payment if there is a dispute concerning goods that were purchased with a credit card

    b. Billing disputes—if a credit cardholder believes that an error has been made by the issuer:

    1.) The cardholder may suspend payment but must notify and give an explanation to the card issuer concerning an error within 60 days of receipt of the bill (in writing)

    2.) The issuer of the credit card must acknowledge receipt of notification within 30 days and has 90 days to resolve the dispute

    c. A credit cardholder will not be liable for more than $50 per card if there was an unauthorized use of the card and notice thereof was given to the card issuer

3. Fair Credit Reporting Act

    a. Upon request, one who is refused credit or employment because of information in a credit bureau report must be supplied with a summary of the information in the report, including the sources and recipients of the information. The individual must be given an opportunity to correct errors.

    b. Consumers have the right to be informed as to the nature and scope of a credit investigation, the kind of information that is being compiled, and the names of people who will receive a credit report

    c. The provider of a credit report must exercise reasonable care in preparing a credit report

    d. Inaccurate or misleading data must be removed from a credit report, and the consumer has the right to add a statement regarding a disputed matter

4. Fair and Accurate Credit Transactions Act of 2003 (FACTA)

    a. Consumers who report suspected identity theft or fraud to a consumer reporting agency must be provided with a summary of their rights at no charge

        1.) The consumer may request that the agency block reporting of information that the consumer has identified as resulting from identity theft

        2.) The agency may decline to comply with the request if the consumer materially misrepresents the information or has received goods or services as a result of the blocked information. The consumer must be notified of the refusal.

    b. Under FACTA, consumers will be entitled to receive a free copy of their credit report annually from each nationwide consumer reporting agency, regardless of being refused credit or employment on the basis of information contained within the report

        1.) The consumer will retain the opportunity to correct errors

5. Equal Credit Opportunity Act—prohibits discrimination based on race, religion, national origin, color, sex, marital status, age, or receipt of certain types of income

6. The Credit Card Accountability Responsibility and Disclosure Act of 2009—established fair practices and helps consumers to better understand the credit transactions into which they enter

    a. Credit card holders must be given 45 days notice of any interest rate increases

    b. Credit cards will not be issued to an applicant under age 21 unless there is a cosigner

B. DEBT COLLECTION

1. The Fair Debt Collection Practices Act prohibits debt collectors from engaging in certain practices

    a. Contacting a debtor at his place of employment if the employer objects

    b. Contacting a debtor at unusual or inconvenient times or, if the debtor is represented by an attorney, at any time

    c. Contacting third parties about the payment of the debt without court authorization

    d. Harassing or intimidating debtor or using false and misleading approaches

    e. Communicating with the debtor after receipt of notice that the debtor is refusing to pay the debt except to advise the debtor of action to be taken by the collection agency

2. Garnishment—a state court may issue an order for garnishment of a portion of a debtor's wages in order to satisfy a legal judgment that was obtained by a creditor

C. IDENTITY THEFT

1. Protection remains primarily in the hands of the individual

    a. Shred papers with personal information before disposal

    b. Do not use links in emails to websites (phishing)

    c. Review billing statements and other financial documents for suspicious activity and report to the vendor immediately

    d.   Before giving out personal information, independently verify identity of

        1.)   Websites

        2.)   Telephone callers

        3.)   Emails

2. Check credit reports for the three primary credit reporting companies regularly for suspicious activity and be alert for changes in the report

    a.   Place a fraud alert on the report if there is suspicious activity

3. Use high quality virus protection and security software on personal computers

    a.   Never enter personal information on public computers

4. Register home and cell phones with the National Do Not Call Registry to limit telephone solicitations (www.donotcall.gov)

D. BANKRUPTCY AND REORGANIZATION

1. Bankruptcy Reform Act of 1978, as amended

    a.   Establishes Bankruptcy Courts with jurisdiction over all controversies affecting the debtor or the debtor's estate

    b.   Provides procedures for the following

        1.)   Voluntary and involuntary liquidation (bankruptcy) of estates of natural persons, firms, partnerships, corporations, unincorporated companies, and associations (Chapter 7)

        2.)   Reorganization of persons, firms, and corporations (Chapter 11)

        3.)   Adjustment of debts of individuals with regular income (Chapter 13)

2. Bankruptcy Abuse Prevention and Consumer Protection Act (BAPCPA) of 2005

    a.   Makes utilization of bankruptcy protection more difficult for debtors who have the capacity to pay; forces many consumers to file under Chapter 13 (adjustment of debts) rather than Chapter 7 (discharge of debts)

    b.   The law also increases creditor protection for retirement accounts to those who declare bankruptcy

        1.)   Under previous legislation, non-ERISA-protected plans (i.e., IRAs) were only protected under state laws that varied state by state. With BAPCPA, most retirement plans are protected in bankruptcy proceedings.

        2.)   Roth and Traditional IRAs are protected up to a $1,283,025 (2016) exemption amount

            a.)   This value changes every three years, with the next adjustment coming in 2019.

            b.)   A ruling bankruptcy body may increase this exemption amount on a case-by-case basis.

            c.)   SEP, SIMPLE, and rollover accounts are not subject to this exemption amount. They have <u>unlimited</u> protection.

    c. The law also outlines certain guidelines for credit counseling and financial education for debtors whose debts consist primarily of consumer debts

3. Discharge of debts (Chapter 7)

    a. Voluntary liquidation

        1.) Commenced by any natural person, firm, association, or corporation (except certain organizations under other chapters)

        2.) Petitioning debtor need not be insolvent unless it is a partnership

        3.) The debtor will be granted an order for relief if the petition is proper and if the debtor has not been discharged in bankruptcy within the past six years

    b. Involuntary liquidation

        1.) Commenced against any debtor, except railroad, banking, insurance, or municipal corporations; building or savings and loan associations; credit unions; nonprofit organizations; ranchers; or farmers

        2.) Creditors who have noncontingent, unsecured claims in the amount of $5,000 or more may file a petition with the Bankruptcy Court

            a.) If there are 12 or more creditors, three of them must join in the petition

            b.) If there are fewer than 12 creditors, one must file the petition

            c.) If a party so requests, a temporary trustee may be appointed to take possession of the debtor's property to prevent a loss

    c. Examples of debt that cannot be discharged under Chapter 7:

        1.) Back taxes (up to three years)

        2.) Debts associated with fraudulent activities, embezzlement, or misappropriation

        3.) Alimony and child support

        4.) Debt due to intentional tort claims

        5.) Student loans

        6.) Consumer debts of more than $650 for luxury goods or services owed to a single creditor within 90 days of the order for relief

4. Reorganization (Chapter 11)

    a. Any individual, business firm, or corporate debtor who is eligible for Chapter 7 liquidation (except stockbrokers, commodities brokers, and railroads) is eligible for Chapter 11 reorganization

    b. A voluntary or involuntary petition may be filed; the automatic stay and entry or order for relief provisions apply

    c. The debtor remains in possession and may continue to operate the debtor's business

5. Adjustment of debts of an individual with regular income (Chapter 13)

   a. An individual debtor who is a wage earner or engaged in business may voluntarily file a petition for adjustment of debts

      1.) The debtor's noncontingent, liquidated, unsecured debts amount to less than a prescribed limit

      2.) The debtor remains in possession of property

      3.) Automatic stay provisions apply

      4.) The debtor submits a plan that may provide for a reduction in the amount of obligations or for additional time within which to pay debts, or both

   b. A reasonable plan that provides for timely payments and is made in good faith will be confirmed by the court. In most instances, the plan will have to be approved by all secured creditors. Approval by unsecured creditors is not necessary.

   c. Most plans call for payments of all or a portion of future income or earnings to be made to a trustee for a five-year period

   d. A Chapter 13 may be converted into a Chapter 7 liquidation or Chapter 11 reorganization

---

ANALYZE AND APPLY

Wyatt has been Brody's financial planning client for two decades. During their annual meeting, Wyatt confided in Brody that his wife of 10 years, Martina, wants a divorce. As a result, Wyatt could lose a large amount of his assets, and he fears he may have to declare bankruptcy due to the high amount of debt he has accumulated. Wyatt tells Brody he understands that if he files for Chapter 7 bankruptcy, some of his debts may still not be dischargeable. Which of the following items may remain Wyatt's responsibility even though he declares Chapter 7 bankruptcy?

A. Credit card debt and student loans
B. Child support and unsecured debt
C. Student loans and debt due to intentional tort claims
D. 5 years of back taxes and alimony paid to his ex-wife from a marriage prior to his marriage to Martina

Answer: C. Credit card and other unsecured debt would be dischargeable if Wyatt declared Chapter 7 bankruptcy. Any back taxes due from periods greater than 3 years ago are also dischargeable. Student loans and debts arising from intentional tort claims will remain his responsibility.
(Domain 3 – Analyzing and Evaluating the Client's Current Financial Status)

XI. INTERPERSONAL COMMUNICATION

CFP Board Principal Knowledge Topic B.14.

CFP Board Principal Knowledge Topic B.15.

A. CLIENT AND PLANNER ATTITUDES, VALUES, BIASES AND BEHAVIORAL CHARACTERISTICS AND THE IMPACT ON FINANCIAL PLANNING

1. Behavioral finance—relates behavioral and cognitive psychology to financial planning and economics in an attempt to understand why people often act irrationally during the financial decision-making process

2. Anchoring—individuals making irrational decisions based on information that should have no influence on the decisions at hand

3. Overconfidence—having an excessively optimistic opinion of one's knowledge or control over circumstances

   Example: believing the investor can do much better than market returns on a regular basis can lead to overtrading, focusing on a single security, or abandoning a previously determined asset allocation

4. Recency—the tendency to emphasize the recent past when considering historical information

5. Herd mentality—tendency of individuals to follow the actions of a larger group, whether rational or not. People who follow the herd often believe that the large group knows something they do not and believe the herd, because so many people are part of it, could not be wrong.

6. Prospect theory—investors generally fear losses much more than they value gains. Accordingly, they will most often choose the smaller of two potential gains if it avoids a sure loss

7. Confirmation bias—people tend to pay more attention to information that supports their preconceived opinions and poorly made decisions, while disregarding accurate, unsupportive information

8. Mental accounting—involves the tendency of individuals to put their money into separate accounts (or money jars) based on the function of these accounts

9. Framing effect—asserts that people are given a frame of reference, a set of beliefs or values, which they use to interpret facts or conditions as they make decisions. Under this theory, people will generally choose what they perceive is positive versus negative, winning versus losing, or getting something of high value versus low value.

B. PRINCIPLES OF COMMUNICATION AND COUNSELING

1. Emotional intelligence—planner must be able to recognize emotional expressions in oneself and the client; also involves the planner selecting socially appropriate responses to the circumstances and client's emotions

2. Active listening—planner should pay full attention to what client says, paraphrasing the client's comments for full understanding of what the client is trying to communicate

3. Leading responses—guide the client to give more detailed responses, making a "meeting of the minds" more likely

4. Body language—involves facial expressions, gestures, and body posture; actually impacts how messages are received more than any other type of communication

5. Context—past history or conditions that exist during communication should be considered by the planner. This includes the client's attitudes, values, biases, cultural influences, age, and expertise. Also, the planner's recognition of his own attitudes, values, biases, and behaviors and the impact they may have on any recommendations made for clients is just as important.

6. Mirroring—accomplished by imitating clients' gestures and physical positions or by using a similar verbal style

   a. Physical mirroring—the financial planner uses the client's body language

   b. Verbal mirroring—the financial planner imitates the client's word use, tone of voice, and communication method

---

EXAMPLE Madison is a financial planner who makes financial decisions quickly. After analyzing and evaluating Evan and Zoey's financial statements, goals, and other information, Madison presents what she feels are several good recommendations for Evan and Zoey, who are conservative and like to consider their options carefully. Madison expected Evan and Zoey to agree to her recommendations without significant delay. In this case, Madison should move away from her own tendencies and give Evan and Zoey adequate time to feel comfortable during the decision-making process.

ANALYZE AND APPLY

Two years ago, you prepared a financial plan for your wealthy clients, Andrew and Caroline. You are meeting them for an annual review of the financial plan. During the meeting, they tell you they would like to liquidate some of their investments to purchase a Ferrari Enzo with another couple next year. Having been a financial planner for years, you know many couples have regretted "wasting" so much money on automobiles. What is the next action you should take?

A. Tell Andrew and Caroline this is a bad idea.
B. Advise Andrew and Caroline how this goal may negatively impact their financial plan.
C. Ask Andrew and Caroline if you can help their friends with their financial planning needs.
D. Refer Andrew and Caroline to your other clients who have purchased expensive cars so they can share their experiences.

Answer: B. You should refrain from giving your personal opinions; however, you should let Andrew and Caroline how this would impact their financial plan. While it would not be unprofessional to ask them to refer their friends to you, this is not the proper time. If you were to refer Andrew and Caroline to other clients who have purchased expensive automobiles, you must make sure you have the clients' permission before proceeding.
(Domain 5 – Communicating the Recommendations)

C.   LEARNING STYLES

1.   Visual—Clients with visual learning styles tend to respond to visual objects, such as graphs, charts, pictures, and reading information. Including visuals in data collection software programs or presentations are beneficial for clients with visual learning styles.

2.   Auditory—Those with auditory learning styles retain information by hearing or speaking. The financial planning process will be most effective if clients' needs, priorities, and goals are discussed before being reduced to writing.

3.   Kinesthetic—Clients with kinesthetic learning styles understand concepts better using a hands-on approach (e.g., writing goals and objectives with bullet points as they are formulated engages clients with this type of learning style)

D.   COUNSELING THEORY

1.   Financial counseling—process of helping clients change their poor financial behavior through education and guidance

   a.   *Economic and resource approach.* Clients are assumed to be rational and will change to the most favorable behavior if given the appropriate counseling. In this approach, the financial planner is the agent of change. The focus is on obtaining and analyzing quantitative data, such as cash flow, assets, and debt.

   b.   *Classical economics approach.* Clients choose among alternatives based on objectively defined cost-benefit and risk-return tradeoffs. The belief in this approach is that increasing financial resources or reducing financial expenditures results in improved financial outcomes.

   c.   *Strategic management approach.* A client's goals and values drive the client-planner relationship. Conducting a SWOT analysis (identifying strengths, weaknesses, obstacles, and threats) is done early in the financial planning process.

   d.   *Cognitive-behavioral approach.* Clients' attitudes, beliefs, and values influence their behavior. Planners use this approach attempt to substitute negative beliefs that lead to poor financial decisions with positive attitudes, which should result in better financial results.

   e.   *Psychoanalytic approach.* Based on the use of psychoanalytic theory, such as Freudian or Gestalt theory, this approach is not widely used by planners.

XII. CFP BOARD'S CODE OF ETHICS AND PROFESSIONAL RESPONSIBILITY AND RULES OF CONDUCT

CFP Board Principal Knowledge Topic A.1.

CFP Board Principal Knowledge Topic A.7.

IMPORTANT: Questions on the national exam will test the CFP Board topics (covered in Books 1–6) in the context of the requirements covered in the CFP Board's Standards of Professional Conduct (the "Standards"). Therefore, you must have an understanding of this material and its application. The following content summarizes the key topics covered in the CFP Board's Standards of Professional Conduct (the Standards). Students are recommended to download the most current version of the Standards at http://www.cfp.net.

A. CFP BOARD'S STANDARDS OF PROFESSIONAL CONDUCT

1. Five sections:

    a. Code of Ethics and Professional Responsibility

    b. Rules of Conduct

    c. Financial Planning Practice Standards

    d. Disciplinary Rules and Procedures

    e. Candidate Fitness Standards

2. Provides principles, rules and standards to all persons whom the Board has certified to use the CFP® marks

3. Upholds the professional standards necessary for proficiency in the financial planning profession

4. All CFP® professionals, including certificants, are subject to CFP Board's Standards of Professional Conduct

    a. Cerficiant—an individual who is currently certified by CFP Board

    b. Professionals Eligible for Reinstatement (PER)—individuals who are not currently certified but have been certified by CFP Board in the past and are eligible to reinstate their certification without being required to pass the current CFP® Certification Examination

5. Use of CFP® certification marks

    a. Certified Financial Planner Board of Standards, Inc. (otherwise referred to as "CFP Board") owns the certification marks CFP®, CERTIFIED FINANCIAL PLANNER™, and the flame logo for the CFP® certification

    b. The CFP® mark must appear in all capital letters and without periods between the letters.

    c. The CFP® mark must be followed by one of the following six approved nouns, except when the mark immediately follows a certificant's name:

        1.) *Professional, practitioner, certificant, certification, mark,* or *exam*

    d. The CFP® mark may not be used as a plural or possessive word.

e. The CERTIFIED FINANCIAL PLANNER™ mark must always appear in all capital letters, or some type of "small cap" font (this is a font that displays all letters of the word capitalized, but makes the first letters of each word slightly bigger).

f. The CERTIFIED FINANCIAL PLANNER™ mark must be followed by one of the following six approved nouns, except when the mark immediately follows a certificant's name:

1.) *Professional, practitioner, certificant, certification, mark,* or *exam*

g. The form of the words in the CERTIFIED FINANCIAL PLANNER™ mark may not be altered or changed.

h. The CERTIFIED FINANCIAL PLANNER™ mark cannot be used as a plural or possessive word.

i. Examples of other taglines and CFP® mark artwork can be found in *CFP Board's Guide to Use of the CFP® Certification Marks.*

B. CODE OF ETHICS AND PROFESSIONAL RESPONSIBILITY

1. CFP Board adopted the Code of Ethics to establish the high principles and standards of the financial planning profession

2. Ethics is a discipline that involves establishing and following moral principles or values

3. The Principles of the Code of Ethics are general statements expressing an ethical and professional model certificants and registrants are expected to follow in their professional activities

4. The Principles represent character ideals and offers guidance to certificants and registrants

5. The Principles expressed in the Code of Ethics are the foundation for CFP Board's Rules of Conduct, Practice Standards and Disciplinary Rules, and together these documents define certificants' and registrants' responsibilities to the general public, clients, colleagues, and employers

6. Seven principles

Principle 1 – Integrity
Provide professional services with integrity.
Integrity demands honesty and candor which must not be subordinated to personal gain and advantage. Certificants are placed in positions of trust by clients, and the ultimate source of that trust is the certificant's personal integrity. Allowance can be made for innocent error and legitimate differences of opinion, but integrity cannot co-exist with deceit or subordination of one's principles.
☑ *Key Points—Principle 1—Integrity*

CFP® professionals must be truthful and open with clients, and they must put the client's interest first, ahead of their own. Because clients trust professionals to guide them on important matters, professionals must display a high degree of integrity as the basis of this trust. This does not mean that innocent mistakes will not occur; financial planning is a practice, and necessitates some subjectivity. However, professionals must always practice with honesty and candor.

Principle 2 – Objectivity

Provide professional services objectively.

Objectivity requires intellectual honesty and impartiality. Regardless of the particular service rendered or the capacity in which a certificant functions, certificants should protect the integrity of their work, maintain objectivity, and avoid subordination of their judgment.

☑ *Key Points—Principle 2—Objectivity*

CFP® professionals must be truthful and unbiased, and make decisions in the best interest of their clients independently of personal prejudices and other predisposed points of view. Professionals must base their opinions and recommendations on sound knowledge of financial planning concepts and experience.

Principle 3 – Competence

Maintain the knowledge and skill necessary to provide professional services competently.

Competence means attaining and maintaining an adequate level of knowledge and skill, and application of that knowledge and skill in providing services to clients. Competence also includes the wisdom to recognize the limitations of that knowledge and when consultation with other professionals is appropriate or referral to other professionals necessary. Certificants make a continuing commitment to learning and professional improvement.

☑ *Key Points—Principle 3—Competence*

Financial planning clients expect CFP® professionals to be both capable and knowledgeable in matters related to their specific circumstances. If professionals lack the expertise in an area of planning that must be addressed by their clients, they should have the insight to refer the clients to another, more competent professional or consult with one. Professionals must also be committed to continuing education in the fields of financial planning, as well as engaging in activities that advance their professional expertise.

Principle 4 – Fairness

Be fair and reasonable in all professional relationships. Disclose conflicts of interest.

Fairness requires impartiality, intellectual honesty, and disclosure of material conflicts of interest. It involves a subordination of one's own feelings, prejudices, and desires so as to achieve a proper balance of conflicting interests. Fairness is treating others in the same fashion that you would want to be treated.

☑ *Key Points—Principle 4—Fairness*

CFP® professionals must have no prejudices when planning for their clients. The relationships with their clients should be based on truthfulness, always making any possible conflicts of interest known to all interested parties.

Principle 5 – Confidentiality

Protect the confidentiality of all client information.

Confidentiality means ensuring that information is accessible only to those authorized to have access. A relationship of trust and confidence with the client can only be built upon the understanding that the client's information will remain confidential.

☑ *Key Points—Principle 5—Confidentiality*

All client information must remain private, as sensitive information is often disclosed to CFP® professionals during the financial planning process. Clients should be made to understand that this information will only be disclosed to authorized individuals. Only through this assurance will clients feel at ease and be willing to divulge all information necessary for completing a sound comprehensive financial plan.

Principle 6 – Professionalism

Act in a manner that demonstrates exemplary professional conduct.

Professionalism requires behaving with dignity and courtesy to clients, fellow professionals, and others in business related activities. Certificants cooperate with fellow certificants to enhance and maintain the profession's public image and improve the quality of services.

☑ *Key Points—Principle 6—Professionalism*

The behavior of CFP® professionals is a reflection of both themselves and their profession. Therefore, CFP® professionals must demonstrate poise and civility to clients and other professionals. CFP® professionals should support one another, always striving to improve and uphold the public's view of the financial planning profession and its services.

Principle 7 – Diligence

Provide professional services diligently.

Diligence is the provision of services in a reasonably prompt and thorough manner, including the proper planning for, and supervision of, the rendering of professional services.

☑ *Key Points—Principle 7—Diligence*

CFP® professionals are obliged to give timely and complete financial planning services. Professionals should consider their clients' specific objectives and circumstances and should make recommendations accordingly. In addition, professionals must manage and follow through any actions needed as a result of the recommendations.

C. RULES OF CONDUCT

1. Set forth the high standards expected of certificants and explains the level of professionalism required of all certificants

2. Binding on all certificants, regardless of their title, position, type of employment, or method of compensation

    a. This is true whether the CFP® marks are actually used

3. Not all rules are applicable to all services provided

    a. Certificants have the responsibility to determine whether specific Rules are applicable to the services they provide

4. Certificants are considered in compliance if they can show that their employer completed the required action

5. Violations may subject a certificant to discipline by CFP Board

6. Rules of Conduct are not a basis for legal liability

1. Defining the Relationship with the Prospective Client or Client

1.1 The certificant and the prospective client or client shall mutually agree upon the services to be provided by the certificant.

1.2 If the certificant's services include financial planning or material elements of the financial planning process, prior to entering into an agreement, the certificant shall provide written information and/or discuss with the prospective client or client the following:

a. The obligations and responsibilities of each party under the agreement with respect to

i. defining goals, needs, and objectives;
ii. gathering and providing appropriate data;
iii. examining the result of the current course of action without changes;
iv. the formulation of any recommended actions;
v. implementation responsibilities; and
vi. monitoring responsibilities.

b. Compensation that any party to the agreement or any legal affiliate to a party to the agreement will or could receive under the terms of the agreement; and factors or terms that determine costs, how decisions benefit the certificant, and the relative benefit to the certificant

c. Terms under which the agreement permits the certificant to offer proprietary products

d. Terms under which the certificant will use other entities to meet any of the agreement's obligations

If the certificant provides the above information in writing, the certificant shall encourage the prospective client or client to review the information and offer to answer any questions that the prospective client or client may have.

1.3 If the services include financial planning or material elements of the financial planning process, the certificant or the certificant's employer shall enter into a written agreement governing the financial planning services ("Agreement"). The Agreement shall specify:

a. the parties to the Agreement;
b. the date of the Agreement and its duration;
c. how and on what terms each party can terminate the Agreement; and
d. the services to be provided as part of the Agreement.

The Agreement may consist of multiple written documents. Written documentation that includes the elements above and is used by a certificant or certificant's employer in compliance with state and/or federal law, or the rules or regulations of any applicable self-regulatory organization, such as a Form ADV or other disclosure, shall satisfy the requirements of this Rule.

1.4 A certificant shall at all times place the interest of the client ahead of his own. When the certificant provides financial planning or material elements of the financial planning process, the certificant owes to the client the duty of care of a fiduciary as defined by CFP Board.

☑ *Key Points—Rule 1*

Material elements of the financial planning process. Note that CFP Board uses the phrase "material elements of the financial planning process" several times in Rule 1. This wording defines the terms of the client-planner engagement, the requirement that an agreement for this engagement be put in writing, the written disclosures that must be made to clients, and the fiduciary duty planners owe to their clients.

Required elements of the financial planning agreement. CFP Board emphasizes the importance of a professional to provide written information or discuss the duties of the professional and the client during all steps of the financial planning process. Compensation that may be received by the professional, any other party to the agreement, or any party legally associated with one of the parties must also be addressed.

If proprietary products are to be presented, terms must be disclosed. Also, if other professionals are to be consulted as part of the financial planning process, terms of these activities should also be made known. Although these matters can be discussed, CFP Board strongly recommends that these conversations be followed up in writing so clients can review the discussion points and have the opportunity to ask further questions.

Requirement of a written agreement. Under Rule 1.3, CFP® professionals are required to enter into a written agreement with clients for any financial planning services or services that include the material elements of the financial planning process. This rule is designed to ensure a "meeting of the minds" between planners and their clients and set appropriate expectations of each party. CFP Board advises that the agreement need not be a single document; separate documents can, say, cover each of the subsections of Rule 1.

Acting in client's best interest. CFP Board stresses the importance of planners understanding their clients' goals, needs, and financial circumstances so that they can act in the best interest of their clients when they make recommendations. CFP® professionals who provide financial planning services or the material elements of the financial planning process are required to do so with the duty of care of a fiduciary, defined as "one who acts in utmost good faith, in a manner he or she reasonably believes to be in the best interest of the client."

ANALYZE AND APPLY

Which of the following are required elements of the financial planning agreement?

1. Terms of proprietary products, if presented
2. Compensation received by the CFP® certificant
3. Any activity of other professionals consulted by the CFP® certificant
4. Duties of the CFP® certificant and the client during all steps of the financial planning process

A. 2 and 4
B. 1, 2, and 3
C. 2, 3, and 4
D. 1, 2, 3, and 4

Answer: D. All of these elements are required. In Rule 1.2, CFP Board emphasizes the importance of a certificant to provide written information or discuss the duties of the certificant and the client during all steps of the financial planning process. Compensation that may be received by the certificant, any other party to the agreement, or any party legally associated with one of the parties must also be addressed. If proprietary products are to be presented, terms are to be disclosed. Also, if other professionals are to be consulted as part of the financial planning process, terms of these activities should also be disclosed. Although these matters can be discussed, CFP Board strongly recommends that these conversations be followed up in writing so a client can review the discussion points and have the opportunity to ask further questions.
(Domain 1 – Establishing and Defining the Client-Planner Relationship)

2. Information Disclosed To Prospective Clients and Clients

2.1 A certificant shall not communicate, directly or indirectly, to clients or prospective clients any false or misleading information directly or indirectly related to the certificant's professional qualifications or services. A certificant shall not mislead any parties about the potential benefits of the certificant's service. A certificant shall not fail to disclose or otherwise omit facts where that disclosure is necessary to avoid misleading clients.

2.2 A certificant shall disclose to a prospective client or client the following information:

a. An accurate and understandable description of the compensation arrangements being offered; this description must include:

i. information related to costs and compensation to the certificant and/or the certificant's employer; and

ii. terms under which the certificant and/or the certificant's employer may receive any other sources of compensation, and if so, what the sources of these payments are and on what they are based.

b. A general summary of likely conflicts of interest between the client and the certificant, the certificant's employer or any affiliates or third parties, including, but not limited to, information about any familial, contractual, or agency relationship of the certificant or the certificant's employer that has a potential to materially affect the relationship

c. Any information about the certificant or the certificant's employer that could reasonably be expected to materially affect the client's decision to engage the certificant that the client might reasonably want to know in establishing the scope and nature of the relationship, including but not limited to information about the certificant's areas of expertise and whether the certificant has filed bankruptcy within the previous five years

d. Contact information for the certificant and, if applicable, the certificant's employer

e. If the services include financial planning or material elements of the financial planning process, these disclosures must be in writing—the written disclosures may consist of multiple written documents: written disclosures used by a certificant or certificant's employer that includes the elements listed above, and are used in compliance with state or federal laws, or the rules or requirements of any applicable self-regulatory organization, such as a Form ADV or other disclosure documents, shall satisfy the requirements of this Rule

The certificant shall timely disclose to the client any material changes to the above information.

☑ *Key Points—Rule 2*

Applying the principle of fairness to understand financial planning services. CFP® professionals are expected to disclose information regarding the services clients can expect to receive and the context in which they will receive these services. As a result, clients will be able to better understand the professional's actions throughout the financial planning process, the basis of recommendations made, and the options available to clients to implement the recommendations.

Disclosure is ongoing. Disclosure does not end at the initial client-planner engagement. As the engagement develops and changes over time, professionals must communicate any resulting material changes to the information in the original agreement. This, too, will allow clients to make decisions based on the most up-to-date information.

Compensation disclosure. Professionals must provide, in writing, clear and precise information regarding all costs and compensation, both direct and indirect, which might result from a certificant's relationships with clients. This applies to both fee-based and commission-based compensation. CFP Board is aware that professionals provide a variety of services and products with many types of compensation structures, and it does not endorse any particular structure.

At first reading, Rule 2.2, which requires that compensation disclosure be in writing, is contradictory to Rule 1.2 b., which allows compensation information to be disclosed either verbally or in writing. There is a subtle distinction here: Rule 1.2 likely relates to activities prior to a financial planning engagement, whereas Rule 2.2 lists the requirements for the engagement/financial planning agreement process.

Disclosing conflicts of interest. Professionals should always place their client's interest ahead of their own and, to this end, should reveal any activities that conflict, or even appear to conflict, with those of the client. If there is any doubt, err on the side of caution; in other words, a professional should disclose the information regarding the transaction.

3. Prospective Client and Client Information and Property

3.1 A certificant shall treat information as confidential except as required in response to proper legal process; as necessitated by obligations to a certificant's employer or partners; to defend against charges of wrongdoing; in connection with a civil dispute; or as needed to perform the services.

3.2 A certificant shall take prudent steps to protect the security of information and property, including the security of stored information, whether physically or electronically, that is within the certificant's control.

3.3 A certificant shall obtain the information necessary to fulfill his obligations. If a certificant cannot obtain the necessary information, the certificant shall inform the prospective client or client of any and all material deficiencies.

3.4 A certificant shall clearly identify the assets, if any, over which the certificant will take custody, exercise investment discretion, or exercise supervision.

3.5 A certificant shall identify and keep complete records of all funds or other property of a client in the custody, or under the discretionary authority, of the certificant.

3.6 A certificant shall not borrow money from a client. Exceptions to this Rule include:
  a. the client is a member of the certificant's immediate family; or
  b. the client is an institution in the business of lending money and the borrowing is unrelated to the professional services performed by the certificant.

3.7 A certificant shall not lend money to a client. Exceptions to this Rule include:
  a. the client is a member of the certificant's immediate family; or
  b. the certificant is an employee of an institution in the business of lending money and the money lent is that of the institution, not the certificant.

3.8 A certificant shall not commingle a client's property with the property of the certificant or the certificant's employer, unless the commingling is permitted by law or is explicitly authorized and defined in a written agreement between the parties.

3.9 A certificant shall not commingle a client's property with other clients' property unless the commingling is permitted by law or the certificant has both explicit written authorization to do so from each client involved and sufficient record-keeping to track each client's assets accurately.

3.10 A certificant shall return a client's property to the client upon request as soon as practicable or consistent with a time frame specified in an agreement with the client.

☑ *Key Points—Rule 3*

Confidentiality is paramount. CFP Board stresses the importance of maintaining the confidentiality of clients' information. This rule also addresses the protection of both physical and electronic information, and emphasizes that professionals should always take wise, practical steps to provide this security.

Need for information. CFP® professionals should strive to get the information and documentation necessary to provide the best financial planning possible. If the required information cannot be obtained, the professional is responsible for advising clients of the inadequacy.

Borrowing money. In general, CFP® professionals are neither allowed to borrow money from clients nor are they allowed to loan money to clients. There are a few exceptions to this directive as listed in Rules 3.6 and 3.7.

Client property. CFP Board goes on to assert that professionals should identify and keep records of all client property taken into their possession. This property cannot be commingled unless authorized by law or unless clients have given written permission to do so. When requested by clients to return their property, they should do so as soon as possible or per the terms of the financial planning agreement.

ANALYZE AND APPLY

1. Gavin, a CFP® certificant, is in the process of preparing a financial plan for Audrey, a 75-year-old widow. For Gavin to properly evaluate Audrey's financial status, Gavin is in need of information regarding Audrey's IRA. Audrey advises Gavin that she does not have this information. Which of the following are actions Gavin should take?

   1. With the help of Audrey, try to obtain the information
   2. Nothing; just proceed with the evaluation without the information
   3. If the required information cannot be obtained, Gavin should advise Audrey of the inadequacy
   4. Discuss with Audrey the IRA values of Gavin's other clients in similar circumstances and come to an agreement regarding the value to use for evaluation purposes

   A. 2 only
   B. 1 and 3
   C. 3 and 4
   D. 1, 3, and 4

   Answer: B. Rule 3.3 requires CFP® certificants to strive to get the information and documentation necessary to provide the best financial planning possible. If the required information cannot be obtained, the certificant is responsible for advising clients of the inadequacy. Therefore, Statements 1 and 3 are correct, and Statement 2 is incorrect. Statement 4 is incorrect because Gavin may violate Rules 3.1 and 3.2 by violating the confidentiality of his other clients if he shares their IRA information with Audrey. (Domain 2 – Gathering Information Necessary to Fulfill the Engagement)

2. Don, a CFP® certificant, has recently encountered serious financial issues due to the costs of medication for his seriously ill child. A number of Don's clients have offered to loan him money until this financial burden eases. From which of the following clients is Don allowed to borrow from without violating the CFP Board's Rules of Conduct?

A. Sarah, a client who works in the medical field
B. Taylor, a client and acquaintance of Don
C. Lance, Don's brother and client
D. Faye, a former classmate for whom Don provides asset management services

Answer: C. Rule 3.6 of the Rules of Conduct disallows a certificant from borrowing money from a client with two notable exceptions: 1) the client is a member of the certificant's immediate family, and 2) the client is an institution in the business of lending money and the borrowing is unrelated to the professional services performed by the certificant. Only Lance falls under one of these categories as he is Don's brother. (Domain 8 – Practicing Within Professional and Regulatory Standards)

4. Obligations to Prospective Clients and Clients

> 4.1 A certificant shall treat prospective clients and clients fairly and provide professional services with integrity and objectivity.
>
> 4.2 A certificant shall offer advice only in those areas in which she is competent to do so and shall maintain competence in all areas in which she is engaged to provide professional services.
>
> 4.3 A certificant shall be in compliance with applicable regulatory requirements governing professional services provided to the client.
>
> 4.4 A certificant shall exercise reasonable and prudent professional judgment in providing professional services to clients.
>
> 4.5 In addition to the requirements of Rule 1.4, a certificant shall make and/or implement only recommendations that are suitable for the client.
>
> 4.6 A certificant shall provide reasonable and prudent professional supervision or direction to any subordinate or third party to whom the certificant assigns responsibility for any client services.
>
> 4.7 A certificant shall advise his current clients of any certification suspension or revocation he receives from CFP Board.

☑ *Key Point—Rule 4*

Manner in which services are provided. CFP Board follows its discussion of confidentiality in Rule 3 with rules that relate the other six ethical principles with financial planning services. All of these principles, when applied, result in the CFP® professional acting within the standard of fiduciary care, acting in utmost good faith, in a manner believed to be in the best interest of clients. This care is to be extended to both clients and prospective clients and includes fair treatment, only offering services for which the professional is competent, meeting regulatory requirements, and exercising sound judgment.

Suitability of recommendations. CFP® professionals are required to make appropriate recommendations to clients. The recommendations should be consistent with client goals and take into account the nature of the client (e.g., risk tolerance).

Notification of suspension or revocation. Should a certificant have his certification suspended or revoked by CFP Board, he should inform his clients.

5. Obligations To Employers

> 5.1 A certificant who is an employee/agent shall perform professional services with dedication to the lawful objectives of the employer/principal and in accordance with CFP Board's Code of Ethics.
>
> 5.2 A certificant who is an employee/agent shall advise his current employer/principal of any certification suspension or revocation he receives from CFP Board.

☑ *Key Points—Rule 5*

Certificants' obligations to employers and principals. In addition to focusing on obligations to their clients, CFP® professionals also have ethical obligations to their employers and principals. CFP® professionals must be dedicated to the lawful objectives of the employer/principal while adhering to CFP Board's Code of Ethics.

6. Obligations to CFP Board

> 6.1 A certificant shall abide by the terms of all agreements with CFP Board, including, but not limited to, using the CFP® marks properly and cooperating fully with CFP Board's trademark and professional review operations and requirements.
>
> 6.2 A certificant shall meet all CFP Board requirements, including continuing education requirements, to retain the right to use the CFP® marks.
>
> 6.3 A certificant shall notify CFP Board of changes to contact information, including, but not limited to, email address, telephone number(s) and physical address, within 45 days.
>
> 6.4 A certificant shall notify CFP Board in writing of any conviction of a crime, except minor traffic offenses, of any professional discipline, or of a change to any matter previously disclosed to CFP Board within 30 calendar days after the date on which the certificant is notified of the conviction or professional discipline.
>
> 6.5 A certificant shall not engage in conduct which reflects adversely on her integrity or fitness as a certificant, upon the CFP® marks, or upon the profession.

☑ *Key Points—Rule 6*

Award of CFP® certification. In order to retain the right to use the CFP® marks, certificants are required to uphold the terms of all agreements with CFP Board. They are also expected to meet all CFP Board requirements to continue using the CFP® marks.

Notification by certificants. Certificants must notify CFP Board of any changes in contact information within 45 days of the changes. CFP Board must also be notified in writing within 30 days of any conviction of a crime with minor exceptions.

Conduct of certificants. Certificants have the responsibility to make sure their behavior reflects the seven Principles of the Code of Ethics for their own sakes, as well as the reputation of their financial planning colleagues and the financial planning profession.

XIII. FINANCIAL PLANNING PRACTICE STANDARDS

CFP Board Principal Knowledge Topic A.2.

A. OVERVIEW

1. Set forth the level of professional practice that is expected of certificants engaged in financial planning

2. Organized based on the elements of the financial planning process

3. Authoritative and provide financial planners with direction

4. Related to the Code of Ethics and the Rules of Conduct

5. Used by CFP Board's Disciplinary and Ethics Commission and Appeals Committee to evaluate a certificant's conduct to determine if the Rules of Conduct have been violated, based on the Disciplinary Rules established by CFP Board

B. PRACTICE STANDARDS SERIES

Practice Standards 100 Series
Establishing and Defining the Relationship with the Client

100-1: Defining the Scope of the Engagement
The financial planning practitioner and the client shall mutually define the scope of the engagement before any financial planning service is provided.

Practice Standards 200 Series
Gathering Client Data

200-1: Determining a Client's Personal and Financial Goals, Needs and Priorities
The financial planning practitioner and the client shall mutually define the client's personal and financial goals, needs and priorities that are relevant to the scope of the engagement before any recommendation is made and/or implemented.

200-2: Obtaining Quantitative Information and Documents
The financial planning practitioner shall obtain sufficient quantitative information and documents about a client relevant to the scope of the engagement before any recommendation is made and/ or implemented.

If the practitioner is unable to obtain sufficient and relevant quantitative information and documents to form a basis for recommendations, the practitioner shall either:
A. restrict the scope of the engagement to those matters for which sufficient and relevant information is available; or
B. terminate the engagement.

Practice Standards 300 Series
Analyzing and Evaluating the Client's Financial Status

300-1: Analyzing and Evaluating the Client's Information
A financial planning practitioner shall analyze the information to gain an understanding of the client's financial situation and then evaluate to what extent the client goals, needs and priorities can be met by the client's resources and current course of action.

Practice Standards 400 Series
Developing and Presenting the Financial Planning Recommendations(s)

400-1: Identifying and Evaluating Financial Planning Alternative(s)
The financial planning practitioner shall consider sufficient and relevant alternatives to the client's current course of action in an effort to reasonably meet the client's goals, needs and priorities.

400-2: Developing the Financial Planning Recommendation(s)
The financial planning practitioner shall develop the recommendation(s) based on the selected alternative(s) and the current course of action in an effort to reasonably meet the client's goals, needs and priorities.

400-3: Presenting the Financial Planning Recommendation(s)
The financial planning practitioner shall communicate the recommendation(s) in a manner and to an extent reasonably necessary to assist the client in making an informed decision.

Practice Standards 500 Series
Implementing the Financial Planning Recommendation(s)

500-1: Agreeing on Implementation Responsibilities
The financial planning practitioner and the client shall mutually agree on the implementation responsibilities consistent with the scope of the engagement.

500-2: Selecting Products and Services for Implementation
The financial planning practitioner shall select appropriate products and services that are consistent with the client's goals, needs and priorities.

Practice Standards 600 Series
Monitoring

600-1: Defining Monitoring Responsibilities
The financial planning practitioner and client shall mutually define monitoring responsibilities.

Julie, a CFP® professional, has signed a letter of engagement with Frank, who is seeking advice regarding college savings plans for his grandchildren. Julie will provide a comprehensive financial plan to Frank in which she will address Frank's college funding goal. Julie has gathered Frank's insurance policies, will, bank statements, and investment reports. Although Frank has disclosed his income to Julie, he refuses to provide her copies of his tax returns or any substantiation of his income. Julie is concerned that Frank is understating his income on his tax returns, and she will not be able to make sound recommendations without his income information. What is the best course of action for Julie to take?

A. Take no further action until Frank produces documentation supporting his income.

B. Julie should approach the IRS to secure copies of Frank's tax returns for the past 5 years.

C. As required by CFP Board's Standards of Professional Conduct, Julie should report her suspicion that Frank is filing fraudulent tax returns.

D. Julie should limit the scope of her engagement with Frank to advice for which she has sufficient and relevant information and, if Frank does not agree to do so, terminate the engagement.

Answer: D. *Practice Standard 200-2: Obtaining Quantitative Information and Documents* requires that, if the practitioner is unable to obtain sufficient and relevant qualitative information and documents to form a basis for the recommendations, the practitioner shall either: restrict the scope of the engagement to those matters for which sufficient and relevant information is available or terminate the engagement. Under the Standards of Professional Conduct, CFP® certificants are not required to report concerns regarding IRS fraud. Julie cannot request copies of Frank's tax returns without Frank's permission. (Domain 2 – Gathering Information Necessary to Fulfill the Engagement)

C. CFP BOARD STANDARDS OF PROFESSIONAL CONDUCT COMPLIANCE CHECKLIST

1. CFP Board provides a checklist as a tool to help CFP® professionals:

    a. document client transactions; and

    b. ensure proper disclosure and compliance with CFP Board's *Standards of Professional Conduct*.

2. See Appendix #2.

XIV. DISCIPLINARY RULES AND PROCEDURES, CANDIDATE FITNESS STANDARDS

CFP Board Principal Knowledge Topic A.3.

A. DISCIPLINARY RULES AND PROCEDURES

1. Used by CFP Board's Disciplinary and Ethics Commission (DEC) to enforce the Rules of Conduct and establish a process for applying the Principles of the Code of Ethics to the professional activities in which a planner (Respondent) engages

    a. Respondent—CFP® professionals (including certificants), candidates for CFP® certification, and Professionals Eligible for Reinstatement (PERs)

2. Reflects the process for applying the Principles of the Code of Ethics to actual professional activities

3. Respondents are given notice of potential violations

4. Respondents have the opportunity to be heard by a panel of other professionals

5. Misconduct by a Respondent, individually or in concert with others, including the following acts or omissions, shall constitute grounds for discipline, whether or not the act or omission occurred in the course of a client relationship:

    a. Any act or omission which violates the provisions of the Rules of Conduct

    b. Any act or omission which fails to comply with the Practice Standards

    c. Any act or omission which violates the criminal laws of any State or of the United States or of any province, territory or jurisdiction of any other country, provided however, that conviction thereof in a criminal proceeding shall not be a prerequisite to the institution of disciplinary proceedings, and provided further, that acquittal in a criminal proceeding shall not bar a disciplinary action

    d. Any act which is the proper basis for professional suspension, as defined herein, provided professional suspension shall not be a prerequisite to the institution of disciplinary proceedings, and provided further, that dismissal of charges in a professional suspension proceeding shall not necessarily bar a disciplinary action

    e. Any act or omission that violates these Disciplinary Rules or that violates an order of discipline

    f. Failure to respond to a request by CFP Board staff, or obstruction of the DEC, or any panel thereof, or CFP Board staff in the performance of its or their duties

    g. Any false or misleading statement made to CFP Board

6. Forms of discipline for Respondents

    a. Private Censure—unpublished written reproach mailed by the DEC to a censured Respondent

    b. Public Letter of Admonition—publishable written reproach of the behavior

        1.) Standard procedure is to publish the Letter of Admonition in a press release or in such other form of publicity selected by the DEC

        2.) If there are mitigating circumstances, the DEC may decide to withhold public notification

c. Suspension

  1.) For a specified period of time, not to exceed five years, for those Respondents the DEC believes can be rehabilitated

  2.) Information regarding the suspension together with identification of the Respondent is often published in a press release or another form as selected by the DEC

  3.) If there are extreme mitigating circumstances, the DEC may decide to withhold public notification

  4.) Respondents who are suspended may qualify for reinstatement to use the marks

d. Permanent revocation of right to use CFP® marks

  1.) Fact of the revocation together with identification of the Respondent is published in a press release or another form as selected by the DEC

  2.) If there are extreme mitigating circumstances, the DEC may decide to withhold public notification

  3.) Revocation shall be permanent

ANALYZE AND APPLY

Matilda, age 62, and Doc, age 68, met with Jack, a CFP® professional, to discuss their retirement portfolio. After conducting a thorough interview, Jack prepared his recommendations. Part of his recommendations was a high-commission bonus variable annuity with a 15-year surrender period. During the interview, the couple indicated that they were concerned about their retirement income and leaving a legacy to their children on a tax-favored basis. The couple took Jack's advice and moved a substantial amount of their assets into the variable annuity. Six months after the transaction, the account was down 12% and they became suspicious of the investment. They had Julie, another CFP® professional, review the annuity and she discovered that this type of contract was clearly not suitable for the couple and that Jack may have acted in his own best interest. Based on this information, which of the following is CORRECT?

1. Julie has a fiduciary duty to notify CFP Board of Jack's actions.
2. Jack may have violated the Principle of Integrity.
3. Matilda and Doc could file a complaint with Jack's compliance department.
4. CFP Board has a legal responsibility to notify a professional's employer in the case of complaint.
A. 1 only
B. 2 and 3
C. 1, 2, and 3
D. 1, 2, 3, and 4

Answer: B. Statements 2 and 3 are correct. Jack may have violated the Principle of Integrity by acting in his own self-interest. Integrity demands honesty and candor which must not be subordinated to personal gain and advantage. Also, he may have violated Rule 4.4: A certificant must exercise reasonable and prudent professional judgment in providing professional services to clients; and Rule 4.5: In addition to the requirements of Rule 1.4, a certificant must make or implement only recommendations that are suitable for the client. The couple could decide to file a complaint with Jack's compliance department, the SEC, and his state's insurance department. Statement 1 is not correct, even though Julie may believe that Jack acted inappropriately, she is not obligated to notify CFP Board. Finally, CFP Board does not have a legal responsibility to contact a professional's employer to discuss the merits of a complaint. (Domain 8 – Practicing within Professional and Regulatory Standards)

B.   CANDIDATE FITNESS STANDARDS

1. Used to ensure an individual's conduct does not reflect adversely on her fitness as a candidate for CFP® certification, or upon the profession or the CFP® certification marks

2. CFP Board determined that such standards would also benefit individuals who are interested in attaining CFP® certification, as many candidates have indicated that if they had known that their prior conduct would bar or delay their certification, they would not have sat for the CFP® Certification Examination

3. The following conduct is unacceptable and will always bar an individual from becoming certified:

    a. Felony conviction for theft, embezzlement or other financially-based crimes

    b. Felony conviction for tax fraud or other tax-related crimes

    c. Revocation of a financial (e.g., registered securities representative, broker/dealer, insurance, accountant, investment adviser, financial planner) professional license, unless the revocation is administrative in nature (i.e., the result of the individual determining not to renew the license by not paying the required fees)

    d. Felony conviction for any degree of murder or rape

    e. Felony conviction for any other violent crime within the last five years

4. The following conduct is presumed to be unacceptable and will bar an individual from becoming certified unless the individual petitions the Disciplinary and Ethics Commission for reconsideration:

    a. Two or more personal or business bankruptcies

    b. Revocation or suspension of a non-financial professional (e.g., real estate, attorney) license, unless the revocation is administrative in nature (i.e., the result of the individual determining not to renew the license by not paying the required fees)

    c. Suspension of a financial professional (e.g., registered securities representative, broker/dealer, insurance, accountant, investment adviser, financial planner) license, unless the suspension is administrative in nature (i.e., the result of the individual determining not to renew the license by not paying the required fees)

    d. Felony conviction for non-violent crimes (including perjury) within the last five years

    e. Felony conviction for violent crimes other than murder or rape that occurred more than five years ago

    © Certified Financial Planner Board of Standards Inc. (reprinted with permission)

Domain Questions

CFP Board's Job Task Domains serve as a blueprint for the CFP® Certification Examination. Each exam question will be linked to one of the following domains, in the appropriate percentages indicated. These domains are based on the results of CFP Board's 2009 Job Analysis Study.

Below are practice questions for Fundamentals of Personal Financial Planning based on CFP Board's job task domains. You can find additional domain-related practice questions in the Volume 7 – Case Book, Online Mock Exam, and the Exam Prep/Review qbank accessible through your student webpage if you have purchased them. For additional information regarding these products, go to http://www.schweser.com/cfp/epr/index.php or call (866) 963-8329.

Domain 1: Establishing and Defining the Client-Planner Relationship (8%)

1. Bob, a CFP® professional, met with Bill and Brenda over a period of six months to analyze and make recommendations regarding their insurance, investments, and retirement plans. Several investments were repositioned to better achieve their objectives and reduce income taxes. In addition, new life insurance contracts were purchased to provide them greater protection. Bob had mentioned in one of the first meetings that he earns commissions on investment and insurance products and occasionally bills for his time depending on the complexity of the work. Following the last meeting, Bob sent a $1,000 invoice to Bill and Brenda for his services. Bill and Brenda objected to paying the fee, saying that Bob should have disclosed his compensation arrangements to them in writing at the onset of the relationship. Bob reminds Bill and Brenda that he did mention how he is compensated in an earlier meeting and that the details need not be in writing because he had not written a financial plan for them. Which of the following is(are) correct regarding the dispute over the $1,000 fee?

    1. Bob has engaged in financial planning and the compensation disclosure should have been in writing.

    2. Bob is correct. He had not provided a financial plan and compensation was discussed verbally; therefore, the compensation details did not have to be in writing.

    3. Although Bob did not engage in financial planning, the compensation information should have been disclosed to Bill and Brenda in writing.

    4. Bob does not have to provide a written financial plan to engage in financial planning.

    A. 2 only
    B. 1 and 4
    C. 2 and 3
    D. 1, 3, and 4

2. Which of the following CFP® professionals would likely be considered to be engaged in financial planning or the material elements of financial planning?

    I.   Bill, who completes a variable life insurance application for Beth, and also reviews the sales brochure with her prior to submitting the paperwork to the insurer.

    II. Katherine, who conducts comprehensive data gathering regarding Jordan's investments, life insurance, retirement plans, wills, and trusts and makes specific recommendations to Jordan.

    A. I only
    B. II only
    C. Both I and II
    D. Neither I nor II

Domain 2: Gathering Information Necessary to Fulfill the Engagement (9%)

1. Ron and his wife Susan, both 61 years of age, ask a CFP® professional to provide a recommendation on whether or not Susan should start to draw Social Security benefits when she first becomes eligible at age 62. Which of the following would be the least important to obtain in order to provide a recommendation? (CFP® Certification Examination, released 08/2012)

    A. Family longevity and health history
    B. Social Security earning statement for each
    C. Other retirement assets or financial needs
    D. Long-term disability coverage

2. A young, single client approaches a CFP® professional with $5,000 stating that he would like to develop a financial plan and invest in the market. This is his first experience investing and he would like help choosing an appropriate account. What is the CFP® professional's most appropriate course of action? (CFP® Certification Examination, released 08/2012)

    A. Open a brokerage account with margin
    B. Open and fund a Roth IRA for the current year
    C. Determine whether the client has any consumer debt
    D. Determine whether the client has adequate life insurance

Domain 3: Analyzing and Evaluating the Client's Current Financial Status (25%)

1. Eli and Sarah, both age 35, have provided you with the following information:

    - Total annual income: $80,000
    - Investments: $28,000
    - Traditional IRA: $20,000
    - Personal residence: $240,000
    - Residence mortgage: $200,000
    - Cash: $4,000
    - Housing payments (P&I): $21,062
    - Housing payments (T&I): $4,000
    - Credit card balance: $25,000
    - Credit card payments: $10,000
    - Student loan balance: $20,000
    - Student loan payments: $5,000
    - Miscellaneous expenses: $4,000

    What is Eli and Sarah's net worth?

    ✓ ⁻A. $47,000
    B. $64,000
    C. $90,938
    D. $131,000

2. Katherine currently has a net worth of $350,000. She is considering the following transactions:

    - Paying a $5,000 debt in full using a gift from a relative   + 5
    - Financing the purchase of a $15,000 home entertainment system on a credit card
    - Purchasing an antique vase, valued at $20,000, for $15,000 with funds from a checking account

    What would Katherine's net worth be after these transactions?

    A. $335,000
    ✗ B. $350,000
    Ⓒ $360,000
    D. $375,000

3. Alyssa, a CFP® professional, is in the process of analyzing and evaluating the financial statements and other relevant information for her client, Bailey. As a financial planning practitioner she gained an understanding of the client's current financial situation. What would be the most logical action that Alyssa should take next?

    A. Alyssa should recommend Bailey consult an attorney to draft any required legal documents.

    B. Alyssa should ask for testimonials and endorsements in order to grow her business.

    C. Alyssa should determine what financial products would be appropriate for the implementation of the financial plan.

    D. Alyssa should determine to what extent Bailey's goals, needs, and priorities can be met by the her resources and current course of action.

Domain 4: Developing the Recommendations (25%)

1. A CFP® professional meets with two new clients who would like advice about their mortgage. In the review, the CFP® professional finds that their essential expenses exceed their income. Mortgage rates have come down significantly and they intend to refinance their current 30-year mortgage to a 15-year mortgage. Their payments will be higher than their current payment. However, they will pay off the mortgage 5 years earlier than the current amortization schedule allows. What should the CFP® professional do? (CFP® Certification Examination, released 08/2012)

    A. Suggest they stay with their current mortgage, as the higher interest is tax deductible

    B. Suggest they refinance to a 30-year fixed mortgage and begin funding savings

    C. Suggest they refinance to the 15-year mortgage, which would reduce the amount of interest paid over the life of the loan

    D. Suggest they meet with their mortgage broker

2. Charles and Kristy have a 1-year old daughter, Isabella. One of their goals is to begin saving today for Isabella's high school education at Greenleaves Academy. After analyzing Charles and Kristy's financial statements and other relevant information, you conclude that they should save $2,000 at the beginning of each year for the next 13 years. Which of the following education planning vehicles is most appropriate for Charles and Kristy?

    A. Section 529 plan

    B. Series EE savings bonds

    C. Traditional IRA

    D. Coverdell Education Savings Account (CESA)

Domain 5: Communicating the Recommendations (9%)

1. Elizabeth, a CFP® professional, is meeting with her clients, Jack and Leah, for an annual review of their financial plan. During the meeting, they tell you they would like to liquidate some of their investments to pay for their daughter's extravagant wedding next year. Having been a financial planner for many years, Elizabeth knows many families have regretted "wasting" so much money on weddings. What is the next action Elizabeth should take?

   A. Tell Jack and Leah this is not a prudent way to spend their money
   B. Refuse to liquidate the investments as this is not in their best interest
   C. Advise Jack and Leah how this goal may negatively impact their financial plan
   D. Ask Jack and Leah if you can help their daughter and her fiancé with their financial planning needs

2. Cole, a CFP® professional, is meeting with his clients, Luke and Marissa, to define their goals. Luke tells Cole one of his goals is purchasing a fishing boat in 2 years, and Marissa rolls her eyes. What is the best action for Cole to do next?

   A. Get more details regarding the purchase of the boat
   B. Ask Marissa if she agrees this is a goal of both Luke's and hers   *Body language*
   C. Ask Luke and Marissa if they have any other goals
   D. Recommend how Luke and Marissa can pay for the boat

Domain 6: Implementing the Recommendations (9%)

1. Joshua, a CFP® professional, started his own financial planning practice 5 years ago. His client, Ryan, approached Joshua asking him for advice regarding a life insurance policy on his own life. Joshua has no expertise in individual life insurance, so he refers Ryan to Caitlin, a local insurance agent and Joshua's daughter. Joshua does not tell Ryan that Caitlin is his daughter. The following week, Caitlin meets with Ryan in Joshua's office to discuss insurance options. Ryan completes an application for life insurance and explains that he does not have the $5,000 annual premium available at this time. Joshua agrees to loan Ryan $5,000, which he repays 2 months later. Which of the following statements regarding Joshua's adherence to the Code of Ethics is(are) CORRECT?

   1. Joshua followed the Principle of Competence by referring Ryan to Caitlin for insurance consultation.
   2. Joshua should have disclosed to Ryan that Caitlin is his daughter to avoid any potential conflicts of interest.
   3. Joshua did not violate the Rules of Conduct when he loaned Ryan money because Ryan repaid the entire balance within 90 days.
   4. Caitlin owes Ryan the duty of care of a fiduciary as defined by CFP Board.

   A. 2 only
   B. 1 and 2
   C. 1, 2, and 3
   D. 1, 3, and 4

2. Alice is a CFP® professional with a growing practice. Several years ago, her client, Joseph, established an irrevocable trust and named his 6 grandchildren as beneficiaries. Joseph is now deceased, but his 6 grandchildren are now Alice's clients. Alice sometimes handles funds for the grandchildren, including distributions from the trust, and the grandchildren often ask her to maintain temporary custody of these funds for periods ranging from a few days to a few weeks. Alice feels it would be convenient to hold all of these funds in a single account rather than setting up a separate account for each grandchild. In which of the following situations is it permissible for Alice to maintain the funds for all 6 grandchildren in a single account?

    I.   If this arrangement is permitted by law.
    II. If each of the 6 grandchildren provides explicit written authorization for this arrangement and Alice has sufficient record-keeping in place to track each client's property accurately.

    A. I only
    B. II only
    C. Both I and II
    D. Neither I nor II

Domain 7: Monitoring the Recommendations (5%)

1. During an annual review with Colton and Stella, Lauren, a CFP® professional, discusses the couple's retirement objectives. Lauren determines Colton and Stella will not be able to meet their retirement funding goals due to weak market performance over the past few years. How should Lauren best direct the discussion of this situation?

    A. Recommend that Colton and Stella increase their monthly savings
    B. Suggest no changes because the market is likely to recover over the long term
    C. Discuss investment alternatives currently available to increase their likelihood of success
    D. Advise Colton and Stella to postpone their retirement date until the economy recovers

Domain 8: Practicing within Professional and Regulatory Standards (10%)

1. James is a CFP® professional whose clients include several small business owners. Some of these businessowners actively seek out new business opportunities to purchase or in which to invest. His new client, Jennifer, also owns a small business. She tells James during their first meeting that she is interested in selling her business on an installment sale basis. Jennifer wants to receive the highest value possible for her business, but she would accept less than market value for the business if necessary to complete a quick sale. If she cannot find an immediate buyer for the business, she would also consider arranging a buy-sell agreement with one of her employees, David, who is also James's client. Which of the following steps should James take first in his relationship with Jennifer?

    A. Gather detailed financial information related to Jennifer's business
    B. Consider alternatives that might meet Jennifer's goals and objectives
    C. Identify and resolve any potential conflicts of interest that may arise in his relationship with Jennifer
    D. Inform his other clients that Jennifer's business is for sale and might be available at a bargain price

2. A client is involved in a potentially litigious matter and asks to confide legally sensitive information to a CFP® professional under the protection of advisor-client privilege. This information may affect another one of the CFP® professional's clients, who happens to be a business partner of the first client. How should the CFP® professional respond to this situation? (CFP® Certification Examination, released 08/2012)

   A. Ensure that the client signs the required Privacy Policy before having any discussions
   B. Caution the client that there is no such thing as advisor-client privilege
   C. Document the information and, as required by CFP Board's fiduciary standard, debrief the second client on the details that pertain to her
   D. Document the information and, as required by CFP Board's Rule on Reciprocal Disclosure

Domain Answers

Domain 1: Establishing and Defining the Client-Planner Relationship (8%)

1. **B**

   Financial planning may occur even if the material elements are not provided to a client simultaneously, are delivered over a period of time, or are delivered as distinct subject areas. Planners do not need to provide a written financial plan to engage in financial planning. Under CFP Board Rule of Conduct 2.2, the CFP® certificant must disclose an accurate and understandable description of the compensation offered, and if the services include financial planning or material elements of financial planning, these disclosures must be in writing.

2. **B**

   Because Katherine's services involve several of the financial planning subject areas, and she is involved in the elements of financial planning, she is likely providing financial planning. Bill's service to Beth is very limited, therefore, the engagement would not be considered financial planning.

Domain 2: Gathering Information Necessary to Fulfill the Engagement (9%)

1. **D**

   Requires consideration of multiple issues such as financial needs, family health history, life expectancy, survivor benefits, and higher wage earner analysis. Disability coverage is not a factor.

2. **C**

   Of the answer options provided, reviewing debt is the best option. The CFP® professional needs additional information from the client before taking an action involving increasing client risk, such as opening a margin account. Reviewing life insurance may be appropriate for the client, but does not appear to be a goal of the client. The CFP® professional does not have enough information to determine if a Roth IRA is appropriate.

Domain 3: Analyzing and Evaluating the Client's Current Financial Status (25%)

1. **A**

   Assets of $292,000 ($28,000 investments + $20,000 IRA + $240,000 personal residence + $4,000 cash) less liabilities of $245,000 ($200,000 residence mortgage+ $25,000 credit card balance + $20,000 student loan balance) equals net worth of $47,000.

2. **C**

   Paying a $5,000 debt in full using a gift reduces Katherine's liabilities; none of her personal assets were used to reduce the debt. This has a positive effect of $5,000 on net worth. Although the purchase of the home entertainment system will increase Katherine's assets by $15,000, the use of credit will increase her liabilities by the same amount; therefore, this transaction has no effect on net worth. Using checking account funds of $15,000 to purchase an asset valued at $20,000 will result in an increase in assets of $5,000 ($20,000 – $5,000). This results in a total net worth of $360,000 ($350,000 + $5,000 + $5,000).

3. **D**

   Under Practice Standard 300-1 (Analyzing and Evaluating the Client's Information), a financial planning practitioner should then evaluate to what extent the client's goals, needs, and priorities can be met by the client's resources and current course of action. At this point, Alyssa should refrain from making recommendations or implementing any action steps.

Domain 4: Developing the Recommendations (25%)

1. **B**

   The clients have a negative cash flow, and should reduce their payments as much as possible and establish a cash reserve.

2. **D**

   Funds saved in Section 529 plans, a Traditional IRA, and Series EE savings bonds may not be used for high school expenses.

Domain 5: Communicating the Recommendations (9%)

1. **C**

   You should refrain from giving your personal opinions; however, you should let Jack and Leah know how this would impact their financial plan. If they still want to liquidate some of their investments, this decision should be documented. This is not the time to ask them to refer their daughter and her fiancé to you.

2. **B**

   Marissa's body language (rolling her eyes) may express that she does not agree this should be one of their goals. Therefore, Cole should clarify whether or not she is on board with Luke's idea. If Marissa is agreeable, Cole should then get more details regarding the purchase of the fishing boat. Cole should not move on to other goals before Luke and Marissa are in mutual agreement regarding this one. At this time, Cole should not make recommendations without more comprehensive information.

Domain 6: Implementing the Recommendations (9%)

1. **B**

   Under the Code of Ethics—Principle of Competence, "competence" includes the wisdom of a certificant to recognize the limitations of his knowledge and to know when consultation with other professionals is appropriate or the referral to other professionals necessary. Rule 2.2 requires certificants to disclose likely conflicts of interest between the client and the certificant, the certificant's employer or any affiliates or third parties, including information about any familial relationships. Under Rule 3.7, a certificant shall not lend money to a client. Exceptions to this rule include: the client is a member of the certificant's immediate family, or the certificant is an employee of an institution in the business of lending money and the money loaned is that of the institution, not the certificant. Neither of these exceptions applies in this case. All CFP® professionals are subject to CFP Board's Standards of Professional Conduct, which contains the Code of Ethics. However, Caitlin is not a CFP® professional, so she is not required to abide by the Standards, which requires fiduciary responsibility.

2. **C**

   Both statements I and II are correct. Under Rule 3.9, a certificant cannot commingle a client's property with other clients' property unless the commingling is permitted by law or the certificant has both explicit written authorization to do so from each client involved and sufficient record-keeping to accurately track each client's assets.

Domain 7: Monitoring the Recommendations (5%)

1. **C**

   All available alternatives should be explored in order to revise their retirement expectations. To make a recommendation before doing so would not be in Colton and Stella's best interest.

Domain 8: Practicing within Professional and Regulatory Standards (10%)

1. **C**

   The first step James should take is to identify and resolve any potential conflicts of interest that may arise in his professional relationship with Jennifer. Potential conflicts exist because of James's relationship with David and the other small business owners.

2. **B**

   Rule 3.1 states "a certificant shall treat information as confidential except as required in response to proper legal process; as necessitated by obligations to a certificant's employer or partners; as required to defend against charges of wrongdoing; in connection with a civil dispute; or as needed to perform the services."

13/16 correct

81 %

Appendix

Appendix 1: Letter of Engagement

Sample Engagement Letter

Rule 1.3 of CFP Board's Rules of Conduct requires a CFP® professional to enter into a written agreement with his/her client if the services to be provided include financial planning or material elements of financial planning. Additionally, Rule 1.3 identifies specific information that must be included in the written agreement.

To assist CFP® professionals in satisfying the requirements of Rule 1.3, CFP Board is providing below a Sample Engagement Letter that a CFP® professional may wish to send to a client at the initiation of a client engagement. Please note that if a CFP® professional elects to use this Sample Engagement Letter, it will be necessary for the CFP® professional to modify the Sample Engagement Letter for each client in order to comply with the requirements of Rule 1.3 and any applicable federal and state rules and regulations.

This Sample Engagement Letter was last updated October 2014.

Name of CFP® Professional
Firm Name
Address
City, State Zip

Date

Client Name
Address
City, State Zip

Dear Mr./Ms. [Client Name]:

Thank you for the opportunity to meet with you. I welcome the opportunity to work with you as your financial planner. This engagement letter outlines the specific terms of the financial planning engagement between:

NAME OF CFP® PROFESSIONAL, CLIENT1 and CLIENT2

If the scope or terms of the financial planning engagement change, they should be documented in writing and mutually agreed upon by all parties to the engagement.

Please be assured that all information that you provide will be kept strictly confidential. During the financial planning engagement, I may, on occasion, be required to consult with other third-party professionals at which time I will obtain your written permission to disclose your personal information.

As discussed during our introductory meeting, this engagement will include all services required to develop a [DESCRIBE TYPE] plan. These services will specifically include: [CHOOSE ANY THAT APPLY –DELETE ANY THAT DO NOT APPLY]

- Reviewing and prioritizing your goals and objectives.
- Developing a summary of your current financial situation, including a net worth statement, cash flow summary, and insurance analysis.
- Reviewing your current investment portfolio and developing an asset management strategy.
- Developing a financial management strategy, including financial projections and analysis.
- Completing a retirement planning assessment, including financial projections of assets required at estimated retirement date.
- Assessing estate net worth and liquidity.
- Identifying tax planning strategies to optimize financial position.
- Presenting a written financial plan that will be reviewed in detail with you. It will contain recommendations designed to meet your stated goals and objectives, supported by relevant financial summaries.
- Developing an action plan to implement the agreed upon recommendations.
- Referral to other professionals, as required, to assist with implementation of the action plan.
- Assisting you with the implementation of the financial plan.
- Determining necessity to revise your financial plan.

This will be an on-going professional relationship. At a minimum, we will meet on an annual basis to ensure the plan is still appropriate for you. [This is not intended to be an ongoing relationship. The engagement will end upon delivery of the services described above.] Either party may terminate this agreement by notifying the other in writing. Any fees incurred prior to date of termination will be payable in full.

My services will be charged on a flat-fee basis [or, describe fees]. We agreed on a fee of $xxx for the first year of service. This includes development and delivery of your financial plan, unlimited email communication and a review meeting in XX 201X. Please provide a check for $$$ with a signed copy of this engagement letter. An additional $$$ will be billed at the end of XX. The balance will be payable [DESCRIBE TERMS]. You agree to pay any outstanding charges in full within 15 days of billing. Please make checks payable to [NAME OF FIRM].

Please be advised that I do not receive a referral fee from any other professionals to whom I may refer you.

[THE FOLLOWING PARAGRAPH MAY BE REDUNDANT IF ADEQUATELY COVERED IN OTHER DOCUMENTS]
In order to ensure that the financial plan contains sound and appropriate

recommendations, it is your responsibility to provide complete and accurate information regarding pertinent aspects of your personal and financial situation including objectives, needs and values, investment statements, tax returns, copies of wills, powers of attorney, insurance policies, employment benefits, retirement benefits, and relevant legal agreements. This list is not all-inclusive and any other relevant information should be disclosed in a timely manner. It is your responsibility to ensure that any material changes to the above noted circumstances are disclosed to me as your financial planner on a timely basis since they could impact the financial planning recommendations.

I have no known conflicts of interest in the acceptance of this engagement. [I am disclosing to you the following conflicts of interest:]. I commit that I will advise you of any conflicts of interest, in writing, if they should arise.

I acknowledge my responsibility to adhere to CFP Board's *Standards of Professional Conduct*, and all applicable federal and state rules and regulations. At all times during this engagement, I shall place your interests ahead of my own when providing professional services. In addition, since this engagement includes financial planning services, I am required to act as a fiduciary, as defined by CFP Board. You can learn more about CFP Board's ethical requirements at www.CFP.net.

I look forward to working with you and helping you reach your financial goals.

Sincerely,

Name of CFP® Professional

CFP® Professional: Client:

I accept the terms of this engagement letter.   I accept the terms of this engagement letter.

_____   _____

Appendix 2: Compliance Checklist

CFP
CERTIFIED FINANCIAL PLANNER
™

CFP BOARD *STANDARDS*
OF PROFESSIONAL CONDUCT
COMPLIANCE CHECKLIST

Client Name: _____   Date Completed: _____

Meeting Attendees: _____

The certification trademark above is owned by Certified Financial Planner Board of Standards, Inc. in the United States and is awarded to individuals who successfully complete CFP Board's initial and ongoing certification requirements.

This checklist is designed to help CFP® professionals document an initial client consultation in accordance with CFP Board's *Standards*. The questions contained in this checklist reflect both the requirements of the *Standards* and established best practices for complying with the *Standards*.

Except for Section A(2), all boxes should be completed for compliance purposes. This checklist should be periodically reviewed throughout the course of your relationship with your client.

Section A: Determining the Scope of the Engagement

1. ❑ **Define the Scope of the Engagement: Rule 1.1, and Practice Standard 100-1**

   Note: After analyzing and evaluating the client's data in Step 2 of Sections B and C, you may need to redefine the scope of your engagement.

   ❑ Have I determined and documented the client's understanding and intent in working with me?

   ❑ Have I determined and documented the extent and breadth of the services I am providing? (See the Personal Financial Planning Subject Areas in the Terminology Section of the Standards)

   ❑ Have I determined and documented the level of data gathering I plan to do?

2. ❑ **Entering into a Client Agreement: Rules 1.2 and 1.3 and Practice Standard 100-1**

   Based on Answers above, is this client a financial planning client?

   ❑ **Yes.** Have I entered into a written agreement (see sample Form FPDA on www.cfp.net) and documented that I have made the required written disclosures (see sample Form FPD on www.cfp.net)? (See Rules 1.2, 1.3 and 2.2)

   Proceed to Section B.

   ❑ **No.** Have I documented that I have orally-made disclosures? (See Rule 2.2)

   Proceed to Section C.

Section B: Financial Planning Engagement Checklist

Note: A CFP® professional shall act in utmost good faith, in a manner he or she reasonably believes to be in the best interest of the client.

1. ❏ **Gathering Client Data: Rule 3.3 and Practice Standards 200-1 and 200-2**

   ❏ Have I determined and documented the client's goals and objectives?

   ❏ Have I documented my discussion with the client of any unrealistic goals and objectives?

   ❏ Have I documented the client data I gathered and any gaps in the data?

2. ❏ **Analyzing and evaluating the client's data: Rules 2.1 and 4.5 and Practice Standard 300-1**

   Note: After analyzing and evaluating the client's data, you may need to return to Step 1 in Section A and redefine the scope of your engagement.

   ❏ Have I documented my analysis and evaluation of the client's data?

   ❏ Have I documented the personal and economic assumptions I used in developing my recommendations?

3. ❏ **Developing and presenting recommendations: Rules 2.1 and 4.5 and Practice Standards 400-1, 400-2 and 400-3**

   Note: You may need to update your disclosures depending on the products and services you are recommending.

   ❏ Have I considered maintaining the client's current course of action?

   ❏ Have I considered and documented appropriate alternatives to the client's current course of action?

   ❏ Have I documented a cost/benefit analysis of the various products?

   ❏ Have I documented how the alternatives are designed to meet the client's goals and objectives?

   ❏ Have I documented how my proposed recommendations are designed to meet the client's goals and objectives?

   ❏ Have I documented my discussion with the client regarding the client's current situation and the rationale for my recommendations?

4. ❏ **Implementing the Recommendations: Rules 2.1 and 4.5 and Practice Standards 500-1 and 500-2**

   ❏ Have I documented the client's acceptance or rejection of my recommendations?

   ❏ Have I determined and documented my responsibility regarding implementation?

   ❏ Have I disclosed and documented conflicts of interest, sources of compensation and material relationships that have not been previously disclosed?

   ❏ Have I selected appropriate products designed to meet the client's goals and objectives?

5. ❏ **Monitoring: Practice Standard 600-1**

   ❏ Have I discussed and documented my role in monitoring the performance of my recommendations?

Section C: Non-Financial Planning Engagement Checklist

Note: *This section represents the minimum standards required of CFP® professionals in all financial engagements. As a best practice, CFP® professionals are encouraged to use the Financial Planning Engagement checklist in Section B in all client engagements.*

1. ☐ **Gathering Client Data: Rule 3.3**

   Note: *Depending on the comprehensiveness of your data gathering, you may need to return to Section A to reevaluate whether you are providing financial planning services or material elements of financial planning services.*

   ☐ Have I obtained all the information necessary to fulfill my obligation to client? If not, have I informed the client of any and all material deficiencies?

2. ☐ **Developing and presenting recommendations: Rules 1.4, 2.2 and 4.5**

   Note: *Depending on the depth and breadth of your recommendations, you may need to return to Section A to reevaluate whether you are providing financial planning services or material elements of financial planning services.*

   ☐ Do my recommendations place the interests of my client ahead of my own?

   ☐ Have I disclosed conflicts of interest, sources of compensation and information that may be material to the client regarding our relationship that have not been previously disclosed?

   ☐ Have I only made recommendations that are suitable for the client?

3. ☐ **Implementing the Recommendations: Rules 1.4, 2.2 and 4.5**

   ☐ Does the recommendation that I am implementing on behalf of the client place the interests of my client ahead of my own?

   ☐ Have I disclosed conflicts of interest, sources of compensation and information that may be material to the client regarding our relationship that have not been previously disclosed?

   ☐ Have I implemented only recommendations that are suitable for the client?

Appendix 3: Tax Tables

2017 Tax Tables

The income and estate tax tables provided by CFP Board for the 2017 examinations were unavailable at press time. Once released by CFP Board, you will be able to find them on the Board's website at http://www.cfp.net/become-a-cfp-professional/cfp-certification-requirements/cfp-exam-requirement/exam-resources/provided-exam-tax-tables. A copy of these tax tables will also be posted on your Exam Prep Review course dashboard in the folder titled *EPR Announcements and Supplemental Documents*.

Appendix 4: Investment Formulas

CERTIFIED FINANCIAL PLANNER BOARD OF STANDARDS, INC.

Provided Formulas

These formulas are available to exam candidates when taking the CFP® Certification Examination:

$$V = \frac{D_1}{r-g}$$

$$r = \frac{D_1}{P} + g$$

$$COV_{ij} = \rho_{ij}\sigma_i\sigma_j$$

$$\sigma_p = \sqrt{W_i^2\sigma_i^2 + W_j^2\sigma_j^2 + 2W_iW_j COV_{ij}}$$

$$\beta_i = \frac{COV_{im}}{\sigma_m^2} = \frac{\rho_{im}\sigma_i}{\sigma_m}$$

$$\sigma_r = \sqrt{\frac{\sum\limits_{t=1}^{n}(r_t - \bar{r})^2}{n}}$$

$$S_r = \sqrt{\frac{\sum\limits_{t=1}^{n}(r_t - \bar{r})^2}{n-1}}$$

$$r_i = r_f + (r_m - r_f)\beta_i$$

$$\alpha_p = \bar{r}_p - \left[\bar{r}_f + \left(\bar{r}_m - \bar{r}_f\right)\beta_p\right]$$

$$T_p = \frac{\bar{r}_p - \bar{r}_f}{\beta_p}$$

$$D = \frac{1+y}{y} - \frac{(1+y) + t(c-y)}{c\left[(1+y)^t - 1\right] + y}$$

$$\frac{\Delta P}{P} = -D\left[\frac{\Delta y}{1+y}\right]$$

$$IR = \frac{R_P - R_B}{\sigma_A}$$

$$EAR = \left(1 + \frac{i}{n}\right)^n - 1$$

$$TEY = r/(1-t)$$

$$AM = \frac{a_1 + a_2 + a_3 + \cdots + a_n}{n}$$

V 2016-01

1425 K STREET NW #800 ■ WASHINGTON, DC 20005 ■ P 800-487-1497 ■ F 202-379-2299 ■ CFP.NET

Provided Formulas (cont.)

$$S_p = \frac{\overline{r}_p - \overline{r}_f}{\sigma_p}$$

$$\sqrt[n]{(1 + r_1) \times (1 + r_2) \times \dots (1 + r_n)} - 1$$

$$_1R_N = [(1 + {_1R_1})(1 + E({_2r_1}))\dots(1 + E({_Nr_1}))]^{1/N} - 1$$

$$HPR = [(1+r_1) \times (1+r_2) \times \dots (1+r_n)] - 1$$

Index

Notes

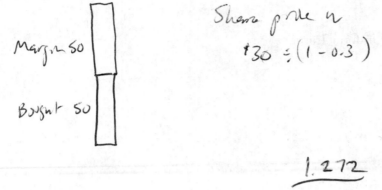

Margin 50

Bought 50

Shere prile n

$30 \div (1 - 0.3)$

$\dfrac{1.272}{.11 - .06}$

32

$37.5 \div (0.6) =$ 62.5

           − 52

$1.5 \times 0.1667 = 0.2501$ $10.5 \times 100 = 1050$

$1.2 \times 0.3323 = 0.4$

$0.9 \times 0.5 = \underline{0.45}$

$0.24 + .75 = .16 = 0.83$

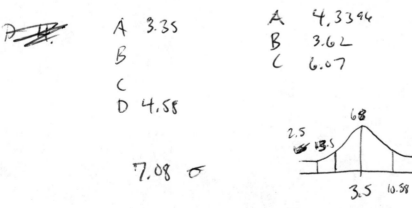

A   3.35   A   4.3394

B   B   3.62

C   C   6.07

D   4.58

7.08 σ

68

2.5

13.5

3.5   10.58

$4.75 = 3 + (6.5)B$

$5.75 = 6.5B$

0.88